Programmed Proofreading
2d Edition

Thadys Johnson Dewar

Professor Emeritus
Department of Business, Vocational, and Technical Education
East Carolina University

H. Frances Daniels

Professor
Department of Business, Vocational, and Technical Education
East Carolina University

Published by

W02 SOUTH-WESTERN PUBLISHING CO.

CINCINNATI   WEST CHICAGO, IL   DALLAS   LIVERMORE, CA

ISBN: 0-538-23020-7

1 2 3 4 5 6 H 2 1 0 9 8 7

Printed in the United States of America

An instructor's manual is available for use with the second edition of PROGRAMMED PROOFREADING. This manual contains quizzes for all chapters, plus five major tests.

PROGRAMMED PROOFREADING, 2d Edition, offers the following special features:

1. Pretest and posttest for students to use in measuring their achievement

2. Simple-to-complex approach to recognizing and correcting errors

3. Emphasis on the use of appropriate proofreading symbols

4. Realistic practice exercises

5. Application of frequently misspelled words

6. Tips to aid in the development of proofreading skills

7. A format that permits students to have immediate reinforcement of learning

8. Special aids in the Appendix

PROGRAMMED PROOFREADING, 2d Edition, provides a thorough review of the rules that a good proofreader must know and a chance to apply those rules through realistic exercises. It is a comprehensive guide for those who would like to develop sound proofreading skills or enhance their present skills.

Preface

Good proofreading skills are essential for anyone whose day-to-day activities rely upon effective communication. Whether a person wishes to improve proofreading skills for business or personal use, PROGRAMMED PROOFREADING, 2d Edition, is designed to assist in the development and refinement of these skills quickly and easily. The text can be used effectively in a traditional classroom, for one-on-one tutoring, or for individual study.

PROGRAMMED PROOFREADING provides a comprehensive review of the rules governing written communication. Proofreading errors and rules are presented in order of increasing difficulty, ranging from simple keyboarding errors to errors in grammar, sentence construction, and content. Realistic practice exercises are provided throughout the text to ensure immediate reinforcement of the principles covered.

Each chapter of PROGRAMMED PROOFREADING concentrates on a particular type of mechanical, format, or content error that a good proofreader must be able to identify. Because spelling is critical to the proofreader, ten commonly misspelled words are listed in each chapter for students to master and apply in the end-of-chapter activities. Tips for strengthening proofreading skills also appear in each chapter.

Three types of proofreading activities reinforce the rules covered in each chapter:

1. Short exercises in which students can immediately test their understanding of a rule or series of rules.
2. A self-check section (usually four paragraphs) at the end of each chapter, in which students can test their comprehension of all of the rules in that chapter.
3. Realistic business documents at the end of each chapter that allow students to test their mastery of the rules they have learned up to that point.

In all cases, students are instructed to use the appropriate proofreading symbols to correct errors.

Three new chapters have been added to the second edition of PROGRAMMED PROOFREADING, beginning with an extra chapter devoted to the elusive "typo" and abbreviation rules. An additional grammar chapter has been included so that students will have a more comprehensive review of sentence structure, subject-verb agreement, pronoun case, pronoun-antecedent agreement, dangling modifiers, and parallel construction. To help students master punctuation, an additional chapter has been included on that topic. Other improvements to the second edition of PROGRAMMED PROOFREADING include a more thorough coverage of content errors, including proofreading for incorrect or missing information, language stereotyping, and redundancy.

Contents

Pretest

Proofread the following sentences for errors and write in your suggested changes. Indicate a correct sentence by writing "C" after it. Each sentence is worth two points. Solutions to the Pretest are on page 213.

1. A number of responses ~~has~~ *have* been recieved from the Febuary 5th mailing.

2. Tom and Julie have gone to the store on Warren road to get five gals. of paint.

3. Bacon and eggs is a traditional breakfast dish in the South. *c*

4. Anséring the telephone and filing ~~is~~ *are* considered routine office tasks.

5. The secretary, as well as the manager, is attending the time-management workshop. *C*

6. Each Kaypro computer and Juki printer ~~have~~ *has* a ~~won~~ *one*-year garantee.

7. Neither Enjou nor Tai ~~are~~ *is* enrolled in Business Law 2142, a graduation requirement.

8. Here are the stationary and the No. 10 envelopes that were omitted from your order.

9. The news bulletin reported that Gen. Arnold's plane would arrive at Kennedy International airport at 10:00 a.m.

10. Their personnel committee *is* reviewing applications for the vacancy.

11. While *I was* running up the stairs, my shoe fell off.

12. The spelling test included these words: quanity, psychology, similiar, and incidently.

13. An artist conveys more than one thought through ~~his~~ *their* paintings.

14. The board voted it's approval of the preformance of the company's officers.

15. Everyone except Leona Peterson and ~~he~~ *him* attended the conference.

16. That lady to whom the award was given said the idea was her's.

17. He gave the following assignment: You must read Life On The Mississippi.

18. The State of Pennsylvania is also known as the Keystone State.

19. A Mid-August survey revealed that many Americans declared French fries to be their favorite food.

20. Installing a computer in our Records Management Department, will increase its efficiency.

21. The clerk was insistant that those 3 sweaters I bought during the Fall sells *sales* could not be returned for any reason.

22. Read chapter five, entitled "Applying for an Executive Assistant's Position," in Wagner's book, *Procedures For The Professional Executive Assistant*.

23. Ms. Dorene Randal, a Yale alumnus, received her m.a. from Duke university, and was recomended for a doctoral fellowship by Dr. D. R. Brandon.

24. the governor of Louisianna flew to the Far East to seek industry for his state.

25. I know that a representative will give ~~his~~ *their* personal opinion whether ~~he is~~ *they are* asked for it *them*.

26. I would like to hire Debbie Ladd who has all ready had two years' experience.

27. Terry, I found three quarters, one dime and twelve pennies—a total of 92 cents.

28. We use the book "Programmed Proofreading" in our introduction to Transcription course, which meets at 9 o'clock each day.

29. Jim's itinerery for Dec. 31, 1987, was completed by 5 p.m. on September 6th.

30. Nine charter members of this chapter of the AMS (Administrative Managment Society) have failed to mail there renewal checks for $110.00.

31. Andy exclaimed, "Stop! The drawbridge is open!"

32. Over 200 of approximately 3,000 customers are behind in their payments.

33. Rhonda says she understnds the 3d economic principal, but she doesn't thing it applies in this case.

34. There will, of course, be a charge for maintainance after the warranty expires.

35. In Chapter 4, Page 14, the following rule appears: Do not divide a word containing 5 or fewer letters.

36. My pruchase came to $3.13, and tax was $.13, making a total of $3.62.

37. You will develop the following skills: listening, transcription and proofreading.

38. The old, dilapidated house will be replaced by a lovely, two-story house.

39. This is where your twin, Don, lives, is it not?

40. In Math 465, 49% of the class failed the final examination.

41. If your voice tends to drop as you utter the expression, then the expression is nonessential; if your voice tends to rise, the expression is essentail.

42. The travel agent said, "Your final payment for the November 1 cruise is due on September 1, thirty days prior to departure."

43. The word "telecommuting" has now become a part of the office worker's every day vocabulary, and should be a familiar term to all involved in the bussiness world.

44. The sign read "Keep the Place Neat," but childrens toys were scattered everywhere.

45. I do plan to take a cruise on the Mississippi River before the cruise company's special expire; however, circumstances prevent me going at this point in time.

46. Twenty-nine of the problems were correct; thats over one half of the total number.

47. Please deliver twelve six-ounce steaks for the party being held at 220 4th Street.

48. Don and Jan's car cost $15,000, and they obtained a loan with 2.9% interest.

49. The letter was signed by Earl Dunn, but the reference initials read "cd:ec." Why?

50. Of all the books you sent me, there was only one I liked—*The Walk West.*

Chapter 1

Proofreading for Quality Control

Objectives: *After completing this chapter, you should be able to*

1. Explain the importance of proofreading in the preparation of business documents.
2. Identify the basic types of errors made by writers and keyboarding specialists in the preparation of documents.
3. List some suggestions for the development of proofreading skill.
4. Utilize the steps in completing the self-instruction exercises in this text.
5. Describe the recommended procedure for proofreading documents.

Importance of Proofreading

Today's office is undergoing vast changes. The high cost of computers and other word/information processing equipment, together with the capability of transmitting information instantaneously to any place on the globe, demands that more attention be given to office productivity and accuracy. Because productivity without accuracy is meaningless, a high level of proofreading skill is vital to the efficient operation of the office or the word/information processing center. Its importance cannot be exaggerated. It has become a "must" for quality control in the office.

To minimize the cost of producing the high volume of documents necessary to meet today's business demands, it becomes imperative that all office workers be able to produce error-free documents consistently. Decisions based upon inaccurate figures can have far-reaching effects on any business. In one instance, an important board of directors meeting had to be canceled after the group had convened when the chairperson noticed a typographical error in the financial report they were to discuss.

Any document that leaves an organization is representative of that firm. In addition to being accurate, the document must be prepared in the correct format and must be perfect in spelling, word division, capitalization, punctuation, expression of numbers, and grammar.

Every document must be proofread carefully. If careful proofreading is not done, a firm's reputation can suffer. The following apology for such an error appeared in a newspaper: "We very much regret our error in yesterday's edition in which we most unfortunately referred to the defective branch of the police force. We meant, of course, the detective branch of the police farce."

The proofreader may be a general secretary, a data entry clerk, a correspondence secretary, an administrative secretary, a supervisor, or a person whose chief responsibility is proofreading. Whether it is done by the keyboard specialist or another employee, proofreading requires a knowledge of English and a skill in detecting errors quickly. This programmed text is designed to help you develop these skills quickly and easily through the completion of a series of related exercises. The programmed format will enable you to check the exercises promptly, thereby providing the immediate reinforcement that is conducive to the rapid development of proofreading skill.

Proofreading Symbols

Proofreading symbols are presented throughout the text as each new type of error is presented. For quick and easy reference, a chart of proofreading symbols is reproduced on the inside back cover of the text.

Kinds of Errors

To become proficient in proofreading, you must be able to recognize errors in mechanics, errors in format, and errors in content or meaning. Skill in detecting and correcting basic typographical errors—such as transpositions, misstrokes, omissions, and number errors—is developed in the second and third chapters of the text. Chapter 4 deals with the basics of word division, and principles of number expression are presented in Chapter 5. Chapter 6 reviews basic letter styles, the correct format for memos, and the principles for arranging reports. As you work through this chapter, you will acquire skill in recognizing inconsistencies in format quickly and accurately.

Once you have acquired skill in detecting and correcting errors in mechanics, you will be ready to concentrate on proofreading for errors in meaning or content. Sentence structure, word choice, and punctuation all affect the meaning of business documents. Chapters 7 and 8 will help you develop your proofreading skills to produce clear and precise written messages. These chapters present basic principles relating to grammatical construction. Agreement of subject and verb, including compound subjects, collective nouns, and indefinite pronouns, is covered. Further, guidelines for the use of pronouns are outlined. Correct word usage, which is vital to clear and accurate interpretation of the message, is explained in Chapter 9.

Because copy that is incorrectly punctuated can cause the content to be misconstrued, the principles governing punctuation are related to content. Chapters 10 through 12 build upon previous chapters by providing principles concerning the use of punctuation marks. The rules of capitalization are covered in Chapter 13. The final chapter deals with content errors related to correctness, redundancy, and language stereotyping. This chapter should help you to further refine your proofreading skills.

Your ability to complete the exercises in the final chapters of this proofreading text will depend upon your mastery of the proofreading principles. This intensive application of all aspects of proofreading should enable you to evaluate your progress and to review specific sections if you need further instruction.

Proofreading Techniques

Proofreading a document usually takes less time than would be required to retype it. You must, therefore, take the time to be a good proofreader.

A good proofreader will usually proofread the copy at least twice. The first proofreading should involve checking for typographical and spelling errors. The second proofreading requires reading the copy to verify the content, format, and grammatical construction. Sometimes a third proofreading may be necessary, particularly if the copy contains statistical information, amounts of money, or long and unfamiliar words.

In order to detect errors when proofreading, you must know what to look for. Using the following techniques will increase your effectiveness as a proofreader:

1. Proofread the document before it is printed or while the paper is still in the machine. If you are using a typewriter, use the paper bail as a guide as you examine each line of copy.

2. Proofread by using the verifying procedure. One person reads the original text aloud while a second person verifies the printed document. This procedure is most useful when checking numbers.

3. To check numbers, run an adding machine tape on both the original and the copy and compare totals.

4. Proofread the copy after you have been working on something else for awhile.

5. Proofread by reading from right to left.

Use of the Self-Instruction Text

You will develop proofreading skill more rapidly and productively if you complete the exercises in proper sequence, filling in all of the blanks and verifying your answers before proceeding to the next exercise.

Beginning with Chapter 2, you will find small units of information (proofreading rules) and short questions in "frames," each of which is numbered and requires a response. Follow these steps in order to complete each frame:

1. Place a piece of paper over the page so only the first frame is exposed.

2. Read the rule(s) and complete each exercise.

3. Slide the piece of paper down and compare your answer with the correct response given in the right-hand column.

4. If your response is correct, continue with the next frame. If your response is incorrect, reread the frame to determine where you erred.

In addition to the numbered frames, each chapter will contain a list of ten spelling words taken from the Frequently Misspelled Words list that appears in the Appendix. So that you can master these ten words, they will appear in the end-of-chapter activities immediately following or in subsequent end-of-chapter activities.

Suggestions for strengthening your proofreading skills are included in the Proofreading Tips section.

End-of-chapter activities include Proofreading Applications and Progressive Proofreading. These sections contain applications of the rules reviewed in the book up through the current chapter. You should be able to identify all errors that apply to the rules learned. Answers to the Proofreading Applications activities are provided in an answer column; answers to Progressive Proofreading activities are provided in the back of the book.

1-1 Proofreading for errors requires careful attention to detail. Find out how adept you are right now at observing detail by completing the following exercise.

Read the following sentence only once and then count the *F*s. Enter your response in the appropriate space.

Fewer Inaccurate Figures are the Result of a Concentrated Effort to Produce Error-Free Copies for the Files.

There are ___6 8___ *F*s in the sentence.

If you counted eight *F*s, phenomenal; the average proofreader spots only six of them. Perhaps you now realize just how easy it is to overlook details.

Proofreading Tips

Study these tips and apply them as you proofread:

1. Develop a critical attitude toward all written communication.

2. Develop your ability to spell. Study the lists of frequently misspelled words given in the Appendix.

3. Be familiar with fundamental principles of word division, capitalization, and expression of numbers.

4. Review the basic principles of punctuation and grammar.

5. Practice reading for meaning.

Remember, proofreading, like keyboarding, requires practice!

Proofreading for Keyboarding Errors

Objectives: *After completing this chapter, you should be able to*

1. Recognize keyboarding errors such as omissions, additions, or misstrokes.
2. Identify errors in enumerations.
3. Use the appropriate proofreading symbols to indicate changes in text.

Omissions, Additions, and Misstrokes

Every word in the English language can be distorted by a keyboarding error. A "typo" (typographical error) results when a typist sees the correct form in the copy but keys it incorrectly. A misspelled word in the original copy is not a typo.

Typos are usually one-letter or one-digit errors. They are often in the form of omissions, additions, or misstrokes. Entire words, sentences, or enumerated items may also be omitted, added, or replaced. Chapter 2 will give you practice in identifying each of these types of errors.

2-1 A letter, character, or space left out of a word is an omission. Entire words or sentences may not be keyed; these, too, are omissions. Use these proofreading symbols to mark errors of omission:

∧   Insert copy.

         was
The child∧thoroughly confus∧d.

\#   Insert space.

Mr. Dees will not attend the/meeting.

Use the appropriate proofreading symbols to mark errors of omission in the following paragraph:

Proofreading is one of∧most valuable skills you can aquire. Like keyboarding, however, proofreading requires patience and pratice. It also requires intense concentration, attention to detail, and mastery of Enlish skills.

2-2 Errors of omission frequently involve closing parentheses, quotation marks, or single letters. In order to locate such omissions, read each symbol or word carefully. Note the difference the omission of one letter would make in these words:

> bridge, bride
> debit, debt
> exist, exit
> the**m**, then, the**y**
> **your**, you

 Use the appropriate proofreading symbols to mark errors of omission in the following paragraph:

Please sign both copies of your contract and return one copy to me. As noted in the contact, you will receive six complimentary copies of your new book. Any addtional copies you request will be debted to your account. (Upon delivery of the first printing, you books will be shipped UPS.

2-3 Adding extra letters, digits, words, or spaces in text is another common keyboarding error. An extra letter may result in a word that *looks* correct but is not. Give special attention to such words as

> country county
> envelope envelop
> interstate intestate

 Also check for words, phrases, or lines that may have been repeated when the text was keyed.

 Use the following proofreading symbols to indicate errors of addition:

⌣ Close up the space.

I can‿not go to school today.

   Delete copy.

There are two err̸ors in this ~~this~~ sentence.

 Use the appropriate proofreading symbols to mark errors of addition in the following paragraph:

2-1

the

of ⋀ most

c
aquire

c
pratice

g
Enlish

2-2

contract
additional
debited
your books
UPS)

Today's word processsing equipment makes the job of editiing much easier than it has beeen in the past. Text can be inserted, inserted, deleted, moved, copied, and searched with merely one or two keystrokes. No longer is it necessary to cut, paste, or start over when revising text.

2-4 Another common error is keying incorrectly, or making a misstroke. Careful proofreading is required in order to find misstrokes in short words such as those listed below:

of, on, or
not, now
than, that, then

Use the symbol below for marking misstrokes:

/   Change copy as shown.

The applicant's persever*a*nce paid off.

Use the appropriate proofreading symbols for marking errors in the paragraph below:

It iw very inefficient to print a document and then decide to proofread if carefully. When errors are discovered at this stage, the work processing specialist must recall the document to the screen, scroll to the proper line and space, correct the error, and them reprint the document. Time and supplies have been wasted.

Enumerations and Tables

Major decisions are made daily on the basis of available figures. Decisions based upon even one incorrect figure can be extremely significant and detrimental. Consider the impact on the financial markets of a $3 billion error in the weekly money-supply figures released by the Federal Reserve in October 1979. The stock market fell sharply as the money-supply figures were released, but the market rallied the following day when the Federal Reserve admitted making the error. The explanation was that "the Federal Reserve clerk who usually compiles the numbers was on vacation, and the substitute failed to spot the error made by a member bank."

2-5 Accuracy is essential when copy includes figures. Incorrect social security numbers, invoice numbers, telephone numbers, amounts of money, and so forth could result in serious consequences. When proofreading copy containing figures, always compare the typed copy digit by digit to the original copy or the source document.

 Mark any errors in the typed list by comparing it to the correct handwritten copy.

Invoice 3478   *$28.72*

Invoice 3693   *$363.20*

Invoice 3649   *$82.02*

Invoice 3700   *$19.20*

Invoices unpaid as of April 30, 1988:

Invoice 3478	$28.72
Invoice 3693	$363.20
Invoice 3695	$82.20
Invoice 3900	$19.10

2-6 Errors frequently occur in the sequence of enumerations (listed items), especially when items are added to or deleted from the list or the list is rearranged. Check to be sure enumerated items are in the correct sequence.

 Use the appropriate proofreading symbols to mark any errors in the following paragraph:

The oldest federal constitution in existence was framed in Philadelphia in May 1787 by a convention of delegates from 12 of the 13 original states (Rhode Island failed to send a delegate). The states ratified the constitution in the following order:

1.	Delaware	December 7, 1787
2.	New Jersey	December 18, 1787
3.	Pennsylvania	December 12, 1787
4.	Georgia	January 2, 1788
5.	Connecticut	January 9, 1788
5.	Massachusetts	February 6, 1788
6.	Maryland	April 28, 1788

2-5

Column A

Invoice **3649**

Invoice **3700**

Column B

$82.02

$19.20

CHAPTER 2—Proofreading for Keyboarding Errors

Spelling Review

Spelling—it's basic; for the proofreader, it's critical. If you have trouble spelling, remember these tips:

1. Develop the *habit* of always spelling correctly.

2. Check a dictionary whenever you are not positive a word is spelled correctly.

3. Pronounce words slowly to be sure you are not missing any syllables (it's *mathematics* not *mathmatics*).

Refer to the list of frequently misspelled words in the Appendix, page 233, as necessary. Approximately ten words from this list will be given at the end of each chapter for you to master. The words in the list below are frequently misspelled as a result of omissions, deletions, or misstrokes. Watch for them in the exercises that follow and in succeeding chapters.

accommodate	congratulations
analyze	consensus
brochure	familiar
changeable	knowledge
commitment	procedure

Proofreading Tips

Suggestions for strengthening your proofreading skills will be included at the end of each chapter. Study these tips and apply them as you proofread. Check closely for the following kinds of keyboarding errors:

1. Omission of letters in long words

2. Repetition of short words, such as *the, and, you,* and *if,* at the beginning of a line

3. Omission of closing parentheses, brackets, or quotation marks

4. Repetition of numbers or letters in a list

5. Omission of words in titles and headings

2-6

Column A

2. Pennsylvania
3. New Jersey
6. Massachusetts
7. Maryland

Column B

December 12, 1787
December 18, 1787

PROOFREADING APPLICATIONS

Proofread the following paragraphs and use the appropriate proofreading symbols to mark any keyboarding or spelling errors. To aid you in proofreading, the number of errors to be found is indicated in parentheses at the end of Exercises P-1, P-2, and P-3. You must find them on your own in Exercise P-4.

P-1 The advent of office automation has greatly impacted on the way communication is created, processed, retrieved (recovered from storage, and distributed. The technologies, how ever, share these common goals:

a. Once information (text, data, or images) is captured, it can be processed by any other technology without recreatinng it.

b. Information can be accessed immediately by those whose work requires it.

c. Information is not printed untill required.

c. Processes are streamlined, thereby improving the organization's abiliy to compete. (6)

P-1

1. storage),
2. however
3. recreating
4. until
5. **d.** Processes
6. ability

P-2 The proliferation of personal computers is having a profound effect on ofice automation. For example, today's knowlege workers are not longer relying solely on secretaries toenter documents. Many originators are keying many of their own documets and are finding that word processing, like the popular spreadsheet software, is but another productivity tool. (5)

P-2

1. office
2. knowledge
3. are no longer
4. to enter
5. documents

P-3 Graphic terminals concert an overload of facts and figures to charts, graphs, and pictures. Users can more easily summarize information or or analize trends when data is in these forms. Engineers can experiment with designs before making a committment. In summary, graphics help users to improve decision making by presenting data in a more meaningful form. (4)

P-4 Electronic message systems (EMS allow short messages to be composed and read at a terminal, thereby reducing the need for a for a paper copy. EMS briges the gap between the slow,physically delivered message and an unaswered telephone. To be effective, a sender must be able to contact who ever is needed, and all users most consistenly check for messages.

P-3

1. convert
2. **or** analyze
3. analyze
4. commitment

P-4

1. EMS)
2. **for a**
3. bridges
4. slow, physically
5. unanswered
6. whoever
7. must
8. consistently

PROGRESSIVE PROOFREADING

The following section provides an opportunity for you to apply your proofreading skills to a job situation:

As office manager for the Superior Insurance Agency, you are responsible for the quality of the documents produced. Sometimes you delegate the responsibility of proofreading to your assistant, but today you are helping out. You have three documents to proofread. Follow the instructions given with each document.

Job 1: File cards prepared from a handwritten list.

Job 2: Memo prepared from a rough draft.

Job 3: Letter transcribed from machine dictation.

Job 1 Proofread the typed cards on the following page by comparing them to the information contained in the memo from Jan Pilgreen, agent, below. Mark any errors you find on the typed cards, using the appropriate proofreading symbols. Check the social security numbers and the telephone numbers carefully.

To: Joan
From: Jan Pilgreen
Date: June 3, 19__
Subject: Index Cards for New Clients

Joan, will you please prepare index cards for the following new clients and arrange them in alphabetical order. Please pay close attention to the soc. sec. and tel. nos. The new filing rules no longer include punctuation with the indexing units (first line).

1. Mrs. Dorothy Brandon
   102 Fletcher Place
   Greenville, NC 27834-5645
   Tel. 919-756-3465
   (255-58-6624)

2. Ms. Grace L. Moran
   106 Brinkley Road
   Dry Fork, VA 24549-5492
   Tel. 703-766-2131
   (277-76-8283)

3. Miss Brenda D. Acevez
   P.O. Box 3066
   Davenport, VA 24239-4392
   Tel. 703-311-4565
   (245-34-5868)

4. Mr. Jerrie Biddinger
   308 Circle Drive
   Crystal Hill, VA 24539-4308
   Tel. 703-456-8121
   (246-66-7790)

5. Mr. John C. Aslakson
   93 Quail Ridge Drive
   Bristol, VA 24201-4019
   Tel. 703-222-9564
   (266-87-9963)

6. Mr. Pat Stallings
   P.O. Box 1901
   Pinetops, NC 27864-0381
   Tel. 919-674-9111
   (244-76-8888)

7. Mr. Henry Stindt
   Route 2, Box 301
   Franklin, VA 23851-7787
   Tel. 804-330-4565
   (258-68-8987)

```
Stindt Henry Mr

Mr. Henry Stindt
Route 2, Box 301
Franklin, VA   23851-7787
Tel. 804-3304565

(258-68-8987)
```

```
Stallings Pat Mr

Mr. Pat Stallings
P.O. Box 1901
Pinetops, NC   27864-0381
Tel.919-674-9111

(244-76-8888
```

```
Moran Grace L Ms

Ms. Grace L. Moran
106 Brinkly Road
Dry Forks, VA   24549-5492
Tel. 703-766-2131

(277-76-8823)
```

```
Brandon Dorothy Mrs

Mrs. Dorothy Brandon
102 Fletcher Place
Greeneville, NC   27834-5645
Tel. 919-756-3465

(255-58-6624)
```

```
Biddinger Jerrie Mr

Mr. Jerrie Biddinger
308 Circle Drive
Crystal Hill, VA   24539-4308
Tel. 703-456-8121)

(246-7790)
```

```
Acevez Brenda D Miss

Miss Brenda D. Acevez
P.O. Box 3066
Davenport, VA   24239-4392
Tel. 703-311-4565)

(245-34-5868)
```

```
Aslakson John C Mr

Mr. John C. Aslakson
93 Quail Ridge Drive
Bristol, VA   24211-4019
Tel. 703-222-9564

(266-87-9963)
```

Job 2 Proofread the memo on the following page by comparing it to the draft copy below. Check to be sure all corrections have been made on the final copy.

June 15, 19--

All Employees

FOUR-DAY WORKWEEK

An experiment in operating on a four-day work week has been approved by the senior officers for implementation on Monday, July 1, through August 31. The procedures below describe the conditions for utilizing our new schedule. *It will run*

1. Operational hours are from 7 :00 a.m. until 5:30 p.m.

2. Each employee is expected to work 9 1/2 hours each day, including three 15-minute breaks. *(Note: An additional break has been added. Department heads will determine break times.)*

3. No less than 45 minutes can be scheduled for lunch.

4. Sick-time policy is unchanged. In case of unforeseeable absence, employees must call in by 8:30 a.m. *may* *e*

5. Casual time allowance (medical appointments, etc.) will be discontinued; the shortened workweek should accommodate your need for personal time. However, if a need exists, it will be up to all supervisors to allow for paid time off.

The four-day schedule will be implemented on an experimental two-month basis. At the end of two months, your feedback will be requested. The senior officers will then decide to continue, modify, or discontinue the four-day work week schedule. *next summer.* *Based on a consensus of employee feedback,*

Jean Quiggins, President

jb

 **Superior Insurance Agency**
14850 Stewart Street
Richmond, VA 23221-5014
(804) 555-7329

June 15, 19--

All Employees

FOUR-DAY WORDWEEK

An experiment in operating on a four-day workweek has been approved
by the senior officers for implementation on Monday, July 1. It
will run through August 31. The procedures below describe the conditions of our new schedule.

1. Operational hours are from 7:00 a.m. until 5:30 p.m.

2. Each employee is expected to work 9 1/2 hours each day, includ-
    ing three 15-minute breaks. (Note: An additional break has
    has been added. Department heads will determine break times.)

3. No less than 45 minutes may be scheduled for lunch.

4. Sick-time policy is unchanged. In case of unforseeable ab-
    sense, employees must call in by 8:30 a.m.

5. Casual time allowance (medical appointments, etc.) will be
    discontinued; the shortened workweek should accommodate your
    needs for personal time. However, if a need exits, it will be
    up to all supervisors to allow for paid time off.

The four-day schedule will be implemented on an experimental
two-month basis. At the end of two months, your feedback will be
requested. Based on a consensus of it, the senior officers will the
decide to continue, modify, or discontinue the four-day workweek
next summer.

Jean Quiggins, President

jb

Job 3 Accompanying this letter is an inquiry card, which supplies address information. Check to be sure the letter address agrees with the address on the card.

Superior Insurance Ag
14850 Stewart Street
Richmond, VA 23221-
(804) 555-7329

```
Abernathy Lucas Mr

Mr. Lucas Abernathy
911 St. Andrews Drive
Fredericksburg, VA  22401-9110
```

June 15, 19--

Mr. Lucas Abernathy
911 St. Andrews Drive
Fredricksburg, VA 22401-9110

Dear Mr. Abernathy

Thank you for your inquiry about our homeowner's policies. You
may choose from either a basic or a comprehensive policy. Should
you desire further coverage, we can also tailor a policy to fit
your specific needs.

Briefly, our basic policy covers losses from the following:

        1. Fire or lighting
        2. Windstorm or hail
        3. Explosions
        4. Riots, civil commotion, or vandalism
        5. Breakage of glass
        6. Smoke
        7. Theft of personal property

Our comprehensive policy covers the above losses in addition to:

        7. Damage from ice, sown, or sleet
        8. Collapse of building
        9. Overflow of water
       10. Freezing of plumbing
       11. Injury from artificially generated current

Each of our policies may be purchases without a deductible or with
either a $100 or a $250 deductible.

Enclosed is a brochre which gives a concise description of each
of these policies and defines each of the above losses. After you
have had a chance to analize it, I will call you for an appointment.

Sincerely yours

Thomas A. Foley, Agent

jb

Enclosure

CHAPTER 2—Proofreading for Keyboarding Errors

Chapter 3

Proofreading for Keyboarding and Abbreviation Errors

Objectives: *After completing this chapter, you should be able to*

1. Recognize transposition errors.
2. Avoid errors by learning to recognize common proofreading symbols used to indicate changes in rough draft text.
3. Apply rules of abbreviation correctly.
4. Use appropriate proofreading symbols to indicate changes in text.

Transposition Errors

One of the most common keyboarding errors is the transposition error. Letters, numbers, words, or sentences keyed in the wrong sequence are called transpositions. When checking for transposition errors, the proofreader should use the following symbols to indicate corrections:

Transpose letters, numbers or words.

These letters must be transposed.

The speaker began to rapidly talk.

3-1 Short words (**ht**e), word endings (*medcial*), and vowels (*thier*) are especially susceptible to transposition. Transpositions can be difficult to detect when proofreading, since a transposition error can result in a word that is familiar but does not make sense when used in place of the original term. Study the following examples carefully:

Geometry is the study of points, lines, angles, surfaces, and solids.

Terry received a letter form Sandy.

Karate, judo, and jujitsu are examples of marital arts.

 Proofread the following paragraph for transposition errors. Use the symbols given above to mark your corrections.

Continued use of electronic workstations can induce eyestrain, stress, and mucsular pain. Consideration must be to given purchasing adjustable furnitrue and to providing workstations with moveable keyboards and adjustable displays. Employee productivity, health, nad job satisfaction are at stake.

Rough Draft Applications

The originator may use certain proofreading symbols to revise text. Typists and word processing operators should learn to recognize and understand these symbols in order to key and proofread text accurately.

Move copy as indicated.

We are invited to a meeting of the Eastern Rockies Purchasing Association.

stet or.... Ignore correction; let it stand.

$15 for the preparation of 100 letters

―――― Change copy as indicated.

before
advance notice prior to the public sale

3-1

mucsular

to given

furnitrue

nad

3-2 Note the use of these symbols in the paragraph below and the manner in which the revisions were made in the second paragraph.

Correspondence can be expensive even without

authors
counting the originator's time. The Fast

Copy Service charged us $15 for the prepara-
tion of 100 letters and envelopes. Additionally, a part-time employee was paid $3
an hour for folding the letters and stuffing the envelopes. They charged us $16.25
for the stationery and the envelopes. By
the time we had paid $22.00 for postage,
this
~~that~~ one mailing had cost us $56.25.

Correspondence can be expensive even without
counting the originator's time. The Fast
Copy Service charged us $15 for the prepara-
tion of 100 letters and envelopes. They
charged us $16.25 for the stationery and the
envelopes. Additionally, a part-time
employee was paid $3 an hour for folding
the letters and stuffing the envelopes.
By the time we had paid $22.00 for post-
age, this one mailing had cost us $56.25.

 Did the typist make all the necessary changes?_____

Abbreviations

Another form of keyboarding error occurs in the proper use and form of abbreviations. Abbreviations are a shortened form of words or phrases used to save time and space. They are generally used in business forms, catalogs, tabular material, footnotes, and bibliographies. Use abbreviations sparingly when a more formal style is desired, as in correspondence or reports.

Debate still exists as to whether periods should be used in various abbreviations. The trend is toward eliminating periods, especially when the elements are capitalized (NATO, TVA). Do not eliminate periods in abbreviations that could be mistaken for words in themselves, such as *in. (inch)*. Although you will find variations in the use of periods, spacing, and capitalization of abbreviations, be consistent within a document.

Space once after the final period of an abbreviation; do not space after a period within an abbreviation (*a.m.*).

When you note errors in the form or use of an abbreviation, use the following proofreading symbols to mark your correction:

(SP)   Spell out.

SP (Adm.) Walker will join us for dinner at 7 p.m.

⊙   Insert a period.

Ms. Jarvis will be present for the briefing.

     Delete the period and close up the space.

Is there an F. D. R. Memorial?

3-3 Spell out first names.

> William (*not* Wm.) Taft
> George (*not* Geo.) Fitzgerald

■ Spell out titles appearing with last names only.

> Senator Proxmire
> General Washington *but* Gen. George Washington

■ Abbreviate personal titles whether used with full names or last only.

Mr.	Messrs.	(plural of Mr.)
Mrs.	Mmes.	(plural of Mrs.)
Ms.	Dr.	

■ Abbreviate titles or degrees after names. Do not set these abbreviations off with commas unless you know that the person addressed prefers a comma be used.

> Dexter Casady II
> James Manchester Sr.

3-2

yes

■ Follow initials in a name by a period and one space. When persons are known only by their initials, no periods are used.

Franklin D. Roosevelt
JFK (John Fitzgerald Kennedy)

 Proofread the following paragraph for abbreviation errors:

Miss Celia Romero and Doctor Wm. J. Cruz will attend the convention in Washington. They have contacted Sen. Paul Morris for passes to the White House. Sen. Morris can also send them passes for congressional hearings of their choice.

3-4 The names of agencies, network broadcasting companies, associations, unions, and other groups are often abbreviated. These abbreviations are usually written without periods. Well-known abbreviations of agency and organization names include the following:

AAA	CBS	NAACP
AFL-CIO	FBI	NFL
AMA	IRS	UN

■ Company names often contain abbreviations such as *Bros.*, *Corp.*, *Inc.*, *Ltd.*, or *&*. Check the letterhead for the proper style. (In some situations, such as in straight text, these words are written in full.)

3-5 Common time designations are usually abbreviated. For example, *A.D.*, *B.C.*, *a.m.*, and *p.m.* Standard time zones and daylight saving time zones are also abbreviated.

EST (Eastern Standard Time)
EDT (Eastern Daylight Time)

3-3

Dr. William
Senator Morris

■ Days of the week and months of the year should not be abbreviated in communications, except in tables, where space might be limited. They may also be abbreviated on business forms.

Wednesday, December 12
On a time card, you could write: Wed., Dec. 12

Use the appropriate proofreading symbols to mark errors in abbreviations in the paragraph below:

Messrs Pena, Adams, and Tonelli have reservations on TWA Flight 22 on Oct. 22 arriving Kennedy International Airport at 1:45 p.m. E.S.T. They will be demonstrating the newest STAR word processing software at the Association of Information System Professionals (AISP) Convention. The camera crews from the educational station W.C.I.M.-TV will be at the A.I.S.P. Convention to tape the presentations for later broadcasting.

3-6   Street addresses are spelled out. Exceptions are the abbreviations *NW*, *NE*, *SW*, and *SE*, which are used in some cities after the street name.

Avenue, Boulevard, Drive, Place, Road, Street, North
1817 Hamilton Avenue, NW

3-4 — 3-5

Messrs.
October
EST
WCIM-TV
AISP Convention

■ Two-letter state abbreviations are used only with zip codes. They are keyed in all capitals without periods or internal spaces. In all other cases, the traditional state abbreviations are used. A list of the state, district, and territory abbreviations appears in the Appendix. Always check these abbreviations carefully in letter addresses and on envelopes.

Name	Standard	Two-letter
Alabama	Ala.	AL
Arizona	Ariz.	AZ
District of Columbia	D.C.	DC

■ Country names are spelled out in text. The exception is *USSR*. When used as an adjective, *U.S.* is acceptable: *U.S.* affairs.

Proofread the following copy for errors in abbreviations:

Nov. 15, 19—

Mrs. H.E.Severson
289 Bershire Ave., NW
Chesapeake, Va. 23320-3456

Dear Mrs. Severson:

Copies of the new software will be shipped to our W. Ger. office. They are scheduled to arrive December 8.

Very truly yours,

3-7 Weights and measurements are spelled out in text but may be abbreviated in technical writing and on business forms.

8 1/2- by 11-inch sheet
9′ × 12′
20 pounds of nails

■ Expressions such as *COD* (cash on delivery) or *FOB* (free on board) are expressed in all caps on invoices and other forms. If they appear in text, lowercase letters and periods are used.

The package was sent c.o.d.

 Proofread the following copy for errors in abbreviations:

April 15, 19—

Mrs. Glenn Martin
1731 Washington Blvd., SE
Little Rock, AR 72201-9581

Dear Mrs. Martin:

Your order of 50 yds. of drapery fabric and 50 yards of lining material is being sent COD today. As the materials weighed over 150 lbs., they were shipped in two cartons.

Very truly yours,

3-6
November 15,
Mrs. **H. E.** Severson
Avenue, NW
Chesapeake, **VA**
West German

Spelling Review

To improve your ability to detect spelling errors, master the words below. Watch for them in the exercises that follow and in succeeding chapters.

believe	environment
committee	February
decision	guarantee
definitely	maintenance
eligible	ninety

Proofreading Tips

Study these tips and apply them as you proofread:

1. Spell out an unfamiliar abbreviation the first time it is used and follow it with the abbreviation: American Management Society (AMS).

2. Although two forms of an abbreviation may be correct, use only one form throughout the same letter or report.

3. When proofreading the work of others, do not assume the original draft is error free. Originators often concentrate more on the content of the document than they do on its mechanics.

4. Compare the final copy word for word with the draft copy and note any differences. Often a word or phrase may be deleted unintentionally as the final copy is keyed.

5. Check the spellings of cities and the state abbreviations in all addresses.

3-7

Boulevard
50 yards
c.o.d.
150 pounds

PROOFREADING APPLICATIONS

Proofread the following paragraphs and use the appropriate proofreading symbols to mark errors you find in spelling, keying, or using proper abbreviations. To aid you in proofreading, the number of errors to be found is indicated in parentheses at the end of Exercises P-1, P-2, and P-3. You must find them on your own in Exercise P-4.

P-1 Are you familiar with hte term *electronic cottage*? It refers to a rapidly expanding group of people using personal computers (PCs) at home for remuneration. Each day thousands of P.C. users complete at least part of their work in the enviornment of their own homes. They may be keying into the main computre at the office, doing freelance work, or writing a book. (4)

P-1

1. **the**
2. **PC** users
3. envi**ron**ment
4. comput**er**

P-2 Personal computers offer many career opportunities fro people who wish to work at home. Providing word processing services, writing software, consulting, and preforming data base research are just a few examples. To attract and maintain customers and clients, operators of cottage industries must provide quality owrk and meet deadlines. (3)

P-2

1. **for** people
2. **performing**
3. **work**

P-3 Every new type of business creates a demand for an organization to serve its needs and interests. So it has been with the electronic cottage people. In response to the rapid growth in the no. of electronic cottage people, several professional organizations have sprung up. Two of them are the National Association for the Cottage Industry (NCAI), P.O. Box 14460, Chicago, Illinois 60614-0460 and the National Alliance of Homebased Buisnesswomen (NAHB), P.O. Box 306, Midland Park, N.J. 07432-0306. (5)

P-4 Did you know that local zoning laws may not permit you to use your home as an electronic cottage? If you make the decision to operate a computer business in your home, you may want to join an organization of electronic cottage people for two reasons: to keep informed and to have a strong, clear voice speaking out on your behalf. One organization taht does this is the Association of Electronic Cottagers (AEC) at 677 Canyon Crest Dr., Sierra Madre, Calif. 91024-1309.

P-3

1. number
2. (NACI)
3. Chicago, **IL**
4. Businesswomen
5. Midland Park, **NJ**

P-4

1. organization **that**
2. Canyon Crest **Drive**
3. Sierra Madre, **CA**

PROGRESSIVE PROOFREADING

The following section provides an opportunity for you to apply your proofreading skills to a job situation:

You are an office assistant in a computer sales and service company. One of your responsibilities is to proofread the materials that are produced to ensure that they are accurate. The three jobs shown below have been given to you for proofreading. Using the proofreading symbols that you have learned, mark all errors.

Job 1: Form letter to all STAR PC users prepared from dictation.

Job 2: A printed list of customers who wish to form a computer users' group.

Job 3: An announcement prepared from a rough draft.

Job 1 Proofread the form letter below to all STAR PC users prepared from dictation.

```
                    February 15, 19--


                    (Letter Address)


                    Dear (Title and Surname)

                    Congradulations!  You are now the proud owner of a STAR
                    personal computer.  We know that you are going to enjoy
                    using it.

                    PC Land offers a one-hour training course to each new
                    customer.  It includes instruction on taking care of your
                    computer, handling diskettes, and copying master disks.

                    A full line of software, including programs for spread-
                    sheets, word processing, file management, and games is
                    available to you at PC Land.  Classes with trained
                    instructors are available with the purchase of any soft-
                    wear package.  Please ask about these classes.

                    Although the STAR has definitly proved itself to be
                    relatively maintainance free, you can secure a service
                    contract customized to your needs.  STAR computers come
                    with a ninty-day warranty and a one-year guarantee on
                    the disk drives.  Our service center honors warranties
                    form other STAR dealers as well.

                    Please call us at 555-2114 or write to us at 125 North
                    First St. should you desire further information.  We are
                    here to serve you.

                    Very truly yours


                    Mr. Tomoko R. Okano
                    Sales Representative
```

Job 2 Printed on the next page is a list of customers who wish to form a computer users group. Check for keying errors in the printed list by comparing it carefully with the handwritten list. Check the printed addresses carefully for proper use of abbreviations; do not assume the abbreviations were listed correctly on the handwritten list.

Customer Names and Addresses

1. Ms. Carmen Alvarez
   4012 Exeter Drive, NE
   Rocky Mount, NC 27801-4439

2. Mr. Davidson Tyler
   1518 Bennett St.
   Washington, NC 27889-6902

3. Mrs. Charles Varlashkin
   P.O. Box 30561
   New Bern, NC 28560-5713

4. Mr. D.L. Pate Sr.
   217-B North Meade Street
   Greenville, NC 27834-4209

5. Dr. Jacqueline Harris
   470 Shoreline Ave.
   Elizabeth City, NC 27909-8261

6. Mr. Christopher Churchill
   1036 Dogwood Trail
   Greenville, NC 27835-3479

7. Mr. Kevin Curran
   8941 Graystone Lane
   Pinetops, NC 27864-2297

8. Ms. Susan Haines
   235 Windsor Blvd.
   Greenville, NC 27834-6140

9. Mr. Jim Gothard
   602 Fairview Drive
   Wilson, NC 27893-4230

10. Ms. Geo. Herndon
    2018 Garrett Avenue
    Farmville, NC 27828-9817

11. Mrs. Valerie Beckman
    301-C Westbrook Apartments
    105 S. 11th Street
    Goldsboro, NC 27530-6346

12. Sen. Jackson
    1442 18th Street, S.E.
    Jacksonville, N.C. 28540-7294

```
Customer Names and Addresses

 1.  Ms. Carmen Alvarez
     4012 Exeter Drive, N.E.
     Rocky Mount, NC  27801-4439

 2.  Mr. David Tyler
     1518 Bennett Street
     Washington, NC  27889-6902

 3.  Mrs. Charles Varlashkin
     P.O. Box 30651
     New Bern, NC  28560-5713

 4.  Mr. D.L. Pate Sr.
     217-B North Meade Street
     Greenville, NC  27834-4209

 5.  Dr. Jacqueline Harris
     470 Shoreline Drive
     Elizabeth City, NC  27909-8261

 6.  Mr. Christopher Churchill
     1036 Dogwood Trial
     Greenville, NC  27835-3479

 7.  Mr. Kevin Curran
     8941 Graystone Lane
     Pinetops, NC  27864-2297

 8.  Ms. Susan Haines
     253 Windsor Blvd.
     Greenville, NC  27834-6140

 9.  Mr. Jim Gothard
     602 Fairview Drive
     Wilson, NC  27893-4230

10.  Ms. Geo. Herndon
     2018 Garrettt Avenue
     Farmville, NC  27828-9817

11.  Ms. Valerie Beckman
     301-C Westbrook Apartments
     105 South 11th Street
     Goldsboro, NC  27530-6346

12.  Sen. Jackson
     1442 18th Street, SE
     Jacksonville, NC  28540-7294
```

Job 3 Proofread the announcement on the next page by comparing it with the rough draft below. Remember, errors may occur on the original document as well. Mark your corrections on the typed copy.

STAR USERS GROUP

Organizational Meeting

You are invited to attend the ~~initial~~ *stet* meeting of the STAR Computer Users Group to be held in the Prince Room of the Tryon Hotel on Feb. 20 at 7:30 p.m.

Anyone using or interested in STAR Computers, software, and STAR-compatible products is ~~encouraged~~ *eligible* to join, so pass this announcement along to your friends.

The STAR User Group will meet monthly to discuss PC-related topics. Guest speakers from industry will share how they are using thier STARS. New products, software, and PC-compatible peripherals will be demonstrated and discussed. All product demonstrations will be video taped and made *chapter* available to members to hear and see. *by the manufacturers. These*

The goal of the STAR Users Group is to provide a network so that all members will be able to use their computers most effectively and to keep manufacturers aware of the consumer's needs.

Members attending the first organizational meeting will determine the best time and location of the monthly meetings and will appoint a nominating comittee for board members.

7:30
Remember: February 20, 8 p.m., Tryon Hotel

Typist - Please set up in an attractive format.

STAR USERS GROUP

Organizational Meeting

    You are invited to attend the initial meeting of the STAR Computer Users Group to be held in the Prince Room of the Tryon Hotel on Feb. 20 at 7:30 p.m.

    The STAR Users Group will meet monthly to discuss PC-related topics. Guest speakers from industry will share how the are using their STARs. New products, software, and PC-compatible peripherals will be demonstrated and discussed by the manufacturers. These product demonstrations will be videotaped and made available to chapter members to hear and see.

    Anyone using or interested in STAR computers, software, and STAR-compatible products is eligable to join, so pass this announcement along to you friends. The goals of the STAR Users Group are to provide a network so that all members will be able to use their computers most effectively and to keep manufacturers aware of consumer's needs.

    Members attending the first organizational meeting will determine the best time and location of the monthly meetings and will appoint a nominating comittee for board meetings.

    Remember: February 20, 7:30 p.m. Tryon Hotel

Chapter 4

Proofreading for Word Division Errors

Objectives: *After completing this chapter, you should be able to*

1. Identify words that are divided incorrectly.
2. Recognize items that should not be divided.
3. Use the appropriate proofreading symbols to indicate changes in text.

Guidelines for Correct Word Division

An important goal of the transcriber or typist is to produce documents that are attractive and readable as well as accurate. To do this, the typist must divide enough words at the ends of lines to maintain an even right-hand margin, yet avoid interrupting the reader with *excessive* word divisions. The typist must also be able to recognize correct and incorrect word divisions when proofreading the finished document. This chapter provides guidelines to help you sharpen your word division skills.

Words can be divided only between syllables. A word division manual or dictionary can be used to determine correct syllabication; however, a knowledge of the rules presented in this chapter will prevent extensive searching in reference materials, reduce word division errors, and save valuable keyboarding time.

Read each of the rules that follow and study the examples given. Then complete the word division exercises. Use the insert hyphen symbol, illustrated below, to indicate the preferred division of each word according to the rule being reviewed (even if a word can be divided correctly at other points). If a word cannot be divided, place a check mark (√) after the last letter in the word.

$$\overset{=}{/} \qquad \text{Insert hyphen.}$$

proof⸆reading

type⸆writer

If a word is divided incorrectly, correct it as shown below.

formal plan of merg⸆er was approved.

4-1   Divide words between syllables only; a one-syllable word cannot be divided.

  height   ac- com- mo-   for- eign
              date

a. careless   d. problem

b. irresistible   e. strength

c. perceive

4-2   Do not divide after a one-letter syllable at the beginning of a word or before a two-letter syllable at the end of a word. An easy way to remember this rule is: Key 2, Carry 3. This means that at least two (and preferably more) letters must be keyed before a word is divided, and at least three letters must be carried to the next line.

  re- cently   print- ers   *but* about or eighty

a. makeup   d. adoption

b. horrify   e. recover

c. brighten

4-3   Divide a compound word between the elements of the compound. If the compound word contains a hyphen, divide only after the hyphen.

  sales- person (*not* salesper- son)   self- esteem

a. get-together   d. bottleneck

b. brainwashing   e. secretary-treasurer

c. fifty-seven

4-4   When a single-letter syllable occurs within a word, divide *after* it. However, divide *before* a single-letter syllable that immediately precedes a terminating two-letter syllable (such as *clar- ify*) or one of these syllables: -ble, -bly, -cle, and -cal.

  apolo- gize   *but* read- ily and prob- able

4-1

a. careless

b. irresistible

c. perceive

d. problem

e. strength ✓

4-2

a. makeup
b. hor- rify
c. brighten
d. adop- tion
e. re- cover

a. benefactor

b. similar

c. gratify

d. eliminate

e. medical

4-3

a. get- together
b. brain- washing
c. fifty- seven
d. bottle- neck
e. secretary- treasurer

4-5 When two single-vowel syllables occur together in a word, divide between them.

situ- ation   valu- able

a. evaluator

b. humiliation

c. anxiety

d. continuation

e. physiological

4-4

a. bene- factor
b. simi- lar
c. grat- ify
d. elimi- nate
e. med- ical

4-6 Divide after prefixes or before suffixes when possible. (A prefix is a syllable placed at the beginning of a word to form a new word; a suffix is a syllable placed at the end of a word to form a new word.)

pre- scribe   friend- ship

a. misplace

b. retroactive

c. introspection

d. arguing

e. kindness

4-5

a. evalu- ator
b. humili- ation
c. anxi- ety
d. continu- ation
e. physi- ological

4-7 You may usually divide a word between double consonants. However, if a word ends in double consonants and has a suffix ending, divide after the double consonants, provided the suffix creates an extra syllable.

hur- ried   press- ing   *but* guessed

a. dwelling

b. recollection

c. embarrassment

d. occurred

e. enrollment

4-6

a. mis- place
b. retro- active
c. intro- spection
d. argu- ing
e. kind- ness

■ When addition of a suffix to a word *results* in double consonants, divide between the two consonants, provided the suffix creates an extra syllable.

occur- ring   permit- ting   *but* equipped

a. deferred   d. concurrent

b. swimming   e. repelled

c. acquitted

Words That Should Not Be Divided

Although most words can be divided, there are some that should not be. The rules for words that should not be divided are stated in the following paragraphs.

4-8   Do not divide a word containing five or fewer letters regardless of the number of syllables. If possible, avoid dividing a word containing six letters.

only   using

a. truly   d. rhythm

b. minus   e. ideas

c. occur

4-9   Do not divide abbreviations, acronyms, contractions, and numbers.

Ph.D.   UNICEF   shouldn't $27,420.15

Exceptions: An abbreviation or acronym that contains a hyphen may be divided after the hyphen.

AFL- CIO

a. o'clock   d. wouldn't

b. f.o.b.   e. 76,000

c. U.S.A.

4-7

a. dwell- ing
b. recol- lection
c. embarrass- ment
d. occurred
e. enroll- ment

a. deferred
b. swim- ming
c. acquit- ted
d. concur- rent
e. repelled

4-8

a. truly
b. minus
c. occur
d. rhythm
e. ideas

CHAPTER 4—Proofreading for Word Division Errors

4-10　Avoid separating parts of a date, parts of a proper name, or parts of an address. If it is necessary to separate one of the above, do so at a logical point.

December 15, 19—	*not*	December 15, 19—
Ms. Carmen Garcia	*not*	Ms. Carmen Garcia
1490 Third Street	*not*	1490 Third Street
Greenville NC 27834-2930	*not*	Greenville, NC 27834-2930
Margaret	*not*	Mar-garet

Proofread the following paragraph using the insert hyphen symbol to correct word division errors.

> Send the boxes of research data to Miss
> Elizabeth Shellenberger. Miss Shellen-
> berger needs the data by September 23,
> 19--, if she is to complete the assign-
> ment on time. Her address is 1542
> Charles Boulevard, Columbia,SC 29202-3169.

4-11　Keep word groups together that need to be read together, such as *6:30 p.m.* and *page 103*. Do not divide the last word of more than two consecutive lines, the last word of a paragraph, or the last word on a page.

Proofread the following paragraph, using the insert hyphen symbol to correct word division errors.

> Thud! That was the sound of *USA*
> *Today* hitting my doorstep at 5:45
> a.m. Quickly I picked up the pa-
> per and dashed back into the secur-
> ity of my home. As I scanned page 1,
> I read with more-than-casual inter-
> est that airline fares are expect-
> ed to decrease in price by Decem-
> ber 1. Just in time for my trip!

Spelling Review

To improve your ability to detect spelling errors, master the words below. Watch for them in the exercises that follow and in succeeding chapters.

announcement	foreign
approximately	height
beginning	nickel
calendar	schedule
category	similar

Proofreading Tips

Study these tips and apply them as you proofread:

1. Pronounce words carefully to determine syllabication.

chil- dren	*not* child- ren
knowl- edge	*not* know- ledge
prob- lem	*not* pro- blem
sched- ule	*not* sche- dule

2. Be alert for words that change syllabication as pronunciation changes.

min- ute	(*n.*) 60 seconds	proj- ect	(*n.*) an undertaking
mi- nute	(*adj.*) tiny	pro- ject	(*v.*) to throw forward
pre- sent	(*v.*) to hand over	re- cord	(*v.*) to write down
pres- ent	(*n.*) gift; not absent	rec- ord	(*n.*) written account

3. Check a word division manual or a dictionary whenever you are in doubt about the division of a word.

4-11

5:45 a.m.
paper
expected
December 1.

PROOFREADING APPLICATIONS

Each of the following exercises contains eight words that have been divided. Some of the words are divided incorrectly or do not follow the preferred style of word division. If a word is divided incorrectly, indicate the correct division by using the symbol for inserting a hyphen.

P-1   commit- ted   permis- sion   para- llel

        begin- ning   gues- sing   embar- rass

        quar- ry   height

P-2   agen- da   vac- cine   refer- red

        alpha- betize   obliga- tion   homeown- er

        tran- slation   simi- lar

P-3   nick- el   commit- ment   do-it- yourself job

        May- 19, 19--   tele- phone   e- liminate

        occur- rence   for- eign

P-4   assign- ment   persu- asion   manip- ulate

        al- ready   gradu- ation   occa- sion

        mid- November   ca- tegory

PROGRESSIVE PROOFREADING

The following section provides an opportunity for you to apply your proofreading skills to a job situation:

You have volunteered your office skills for five hours a week to Partners, Inc., a local charitable organization. Because you are a good proofreader, you are often asked to check the work of others.

Today your in-basket contains three items. Proofread them carefully for keyboarding, spelling, and word division errors. Remember, the original drafts may also contain errors.

Job 1: A memo and news release to be sent to radio stations.

Job 2: Schedule of volunteers prepared from a handwritten list.

Job 3: Form letter to be sent to Partners, Inc.'s supporters. It was prepared from a rough draft.

P-1

1. quarry
2. guess- ing
3. paral- lel

P-2

1. agenda
2. trans- lation
3. referred
4. home- owner

P-3

1. nickel
2. May 19,
3. elimi- nate

P-4

1. persua- sion
2. cate- gory
3. manipu- late

Partners, Inc.

1110 Logan Street
Denver, CO 80203-9176   (303) 555-6478

January 10, 19--

Pat Hamilton, Station Manager

PUBLIC ANNOUNCMENT

For the past four years, your station has very generously adver-
tised the Partners' Auction as a public service announcement. The
Partners' Auction is held annually to raise money to support projects for the youth in our community. Can we count on your continued support this year?

If your response is Yes, and we hope it will be, would you please
read the news release that is enclosed over the air begining January
29 and running through Febuary 5.

Joseph A. Ramirez, Executive Secretary

re

Enclosure

Partners, Inc.

1110 Logan Street
Denver, CO 80203-9176
(303) 555-6478

NEWS RELEASE

January 10, 19--

For Release January 29, 19--

FIFTH ANNUAL PARTNERS' ACUTION

The Fifth Annual Partners' Auction will be telecast on W.R.-A.L.-T.V. from noon to midnight on Saturday, February 5. Local merchants have generously donated aproximately 1,575 gifts. You can bid on any of them by calling one of the numbers listed on your television screen. The retail value will be given for each item, and it will be sold to the highest bidder. All persons working with the auction donate their time; thus all proceeds go directly to Partners to aid the youth of our community.

###

Job 2 Proofread the schedule on the following page by comparing it to the sign-up sheet below. Check to be sure that names on the sign-up sheet have not been omitted from the typed schedule. Also check to be sure that the typist alphabetized the names.

BULLETIN

SIGN-UP SHEET

PARTNERS' AUCTION

Scott Pavilion

Saturday, February 5, 19--

*Typist—
Please
alphabetize
these names
J.R.*

Please sign up for the time you would like to work at the auction.
Plan to be present 15 minutes before your assigned starting time.

<u>12 noon to 3 p.m.</u>

Suzanne Trifunovic
Rhonda Wood
George Yan
David C. Thomas

<u>3 p.m. to 5 p.m.</u>

Sharon Kennedy
Scott Smith
Winton Woodard
Rodney Dibble
Edward McMillan

<u>6 p.m. to 9 p.m.</u>

Clement Nelson
June Shavitz
Terry Boiter
Joseph Fuller
Eileen DeForge

<u>9 p.m. to 12 midnight</u>

Leslie Hagan
Woodrow Windstead
Marie Parrish
Kimberly Popatak
Janie White

BULLETIN

PARTNERS' AUCTION
Scott Pavilion
Saturday, February 5, 19--

Here is the work schedual for the Partners' Auction. To assure
that each shift is replaced promptly, please arrive at the Pavilion 15 minutes before you assigned starting time.

<u>Time</u>	<u>Volunteers</u>
12 noon to 3 p.m.	David C. Thomas Suzanne Trifunovic Rhonda Wood George Yon
3 p.m. to 5 p.m.	Rodney Dibble Sharon Kennedy Edward McMillan Winton Woodard
6 p.m. to 9 p.m.	Terry Boiter Eileen Deforge Joseph Fuller Clement Nelson June Shavitz
9 p.m. to 12 midnight	Leslie Hagan Marie Parrish Kimberly Popatak Woodrow Windstead Janie White

Job 3 Proofread the form letter on the following page by comparing it to the rough draft below. Check for keyboarding, spelling, and word division errors. Remember, errors may occur in the draft copy as well.

Typist:
Please prepare in
proper form

January 15, 19--

(Letter Address)

As a loyal supporter of Partners, you know how vital

Ladies and Gentlemen

Mark your calender for the Fifth Annual Partner's Auction to be held on Saturday, February 5, in Scott Pavilion. The auction is sponsored by area businesses for the benefit of Partners, Inc., an organization devoted to helping the youth of the community. Since you are aware of the importance of the auction *is* as a means of raising funds for the organization you will want to attend.

WRAL-TV will telecast the auction from noon to midnigth. As each item is put up for bid, it will be shown on television and its retail value will be given. You can place your bid for any item by calling the numbers listed on the *stet* television *stet* screen. Remember, too, that *should* if your bid is *be for* more than the retail value of the item, the difference between the two amounts is tax deductible on your taxes.

We hope that you will make a definite decsion to participate in Partners' biggest fund-raiser of the year. When Partners benefits, the entire community benefits.

Sincerely yours

Joseph A. Ramirez

Executive Secretary

Persons working at the auction are volunteering their services; therefore, all proceeds go directly to Partners.

January 15, 19--

(Letter Address)

Ladies and Gentlemen

Mark your calender for the Fifth Annaul Partners' Auction
to be held on Saturday, February 5, in Scott Pavilion.
The auction is sponsored by area buisnesses for the benefit of Partners, Inc., an organization devoted to helping the youth of the community. As a loyal supporter of
Partners, you know how vital the auction is as a means of
raising funds for the organization.

WRAL-TV will telecast the action from noon to midnight.
As each item is put up for bid, it will be shown on television, and its retail value will be given. You can
place your bid for any item by calling the numbers listed on television. Should your bit be for more than the
retail value, the difference between the two is deductible on your taxes.

Persons working at the auction are volunteering their
services; therefore, all proceeds go directly to Partners.
We hope you will participate in Partners' biggest fund-
raiser of the year. When Partners benefits, the entire
community benefits.

Sincerely yours

Joseph A. Ramirez
Executive Secretary

re

Chapter 5

Proofreading for Errors in Expression of Numbers

Objectives: *After completing this chapter, you should be able to*

1. Identify errors in the expression of numbers.
2. Identify errors in numerical calculations resulting from keyboarding.
3. Use appropriate proofreading symbols to indicate changes in text.

General Guidelines

An important aspect of developing proofreading skills is learning to detect errors in the expression of numbers. Because of the availability of vast amounts of information from computers, numbers occur frequently in business documents. Much of the information is of a statistical nature. Thus, the proofreader must take extra precautions to locate errors in the expression of numbers and statistical errors.

Because figures are quickly and easily perceived, numbers used in technical writing and business communication are usually expressed in figures. On the other hand, numbers used in formal documents such as social invitations are often spelled out. While authorities do not agree on the rules in all cases, there are some generally accepted guidelines that are to be followed in business communication. The rules presented in Chapter 5 apply to the expression of numbers as they appear in business documents unless otherwise noted.

Use the following proofreading symbols to mark errors in the expression of numbers and in the calculation of numerical items:

(SP)   Spell out.

We enrolled (10) students in the proofreading class.

———   Change copy as indicated.

The nurse prepared 10 bandages, ~~five~~ 5 rolls of gauze, and 20 tongue depressors.

The first part of Chapter 5 deals with basic rules for expressing numbers in business communication. Because these are basic rules for expressing numbers, the proofreader must be thoroughly familiar with each one.

5-1 Write the numbers one through ten in words. Write numbers larger than ten in figures.

> It takes five years to qualify for membership.

> It takes 12 years to qualify for membership.

5-2 If a sentence contains a series of numbers, any of which is over ten, use figures for consistency.

> For the picnic, they bought 24 pounds of chopped beef, 8 dozen rolls, 36 quarts of lemonade, and 96 turnovers.

■ If the numbers in a sentence can be grouped into different categories, examine each category separately. If figures are required for some numbers in a given category, use figures for all numbers within that category. (Categories may include numbers in a series, round numbers, ordinal numbers, dates, time, money, percentages, etc.)

The Per-Flo tour registered 37 women, 28 men, and 5 children for the *three* tours offered.

5-3 Always spell out a number that begins a sentence. When possible rearrange the sentence so that it does not begin with a number. (Note: The numbers twenty-one through ninety-nine should always be hyphenated when spelled out.)

> Twenty-five persons have enrolled.

not Seven hundred eighty-nine was the number of the lucky ticket.

but The number of the lucky ticket was 789.

5-4 Spell out indefinite (or round) numbers that can be expressed in one or two words.

> About three thousand people attended the rally.

> Approximately fifty men entered the contest.

- Express round numbers such as 1,500 in hundreds rather than thousands.

> fifteen hundred balloons
>
> *not*   one thousand five hundred balloons

- Express very large round numbers in figures followed by the word *million* or *billion*.

> The population of Chicago is over 3 million.

5-5 Spell out ordinal numbers that can be written in one or two words. (Count hyphenated numbers such as thirty-five as one word.)

> Is this the sixth inning?

> Harold and Sue celebrated their forty-fifth anniversary.

- If an ordinal number cannot be expressed in one or two words, use figures.

> This is the 110th day of the strike.

 Proofread the following sentences for errors in the expression of numbers. If the sentence is correct, write a *C* to the right of the sentence.

a. The publisher has 5 branch offices and 3 warehouses.

b. Our office employs 24 full-time and 6 part-time people, but there are more than two million federal employees.

c. There were about one thousand four hundred people at the convention.

d. 102 errors were found in the report!

e. Mark ranked fourth in a class of 75.

f. This is Pat's fifth year with the company.

Guidelines for Specific Situations

Specific situations require additional guidelines to clarify the message. These rules are covered in this section.

5-6 When two numbers are used together and one is part of a compound modifier, spell out the smaller number and write the larger number in figures.

> Calvin loaded two 40-pound cartons on the truck.
>
> Martha bought 20 three-cent stamps.

5-7 Spell out street names of ten or less and the house number *one*. Street names of ten and under are always expressed as ordinals (Third Street, Fifth Street). Street names above ten may be expressed in figures as cardinal numbers (15 Street) or as ordinal numbers (15th Street).

> 1609 Fifth Avenue
>
> One Park Avenue
>
> 2109 Sandcastle Drive
>
> 2 East 11th Street (or 2 East 11 Street)

5-8 Spell out ages unless expressed in years and months.

> When will Chris be twenty-one?
>
> Jim is 3 years and 9 months old.

5-9 Use figures to express numbers preceded by nouns.

Please refer to page 16 in Chapter 2 when you do your research.
The meeting will be held in Suite 101.

5-1—5-5

a. ⑤ *sp* branch offices and ③ *sp*
   warehouses

b. ~~two~~ *2* million

c. ~~one thousand four~~ *fourteen*
   ~~hundred~~

d. ~~102~~ *One hundred two*

e. C

f. C

Proofread the following sentences for errors in the expression of numbers.

  a. Mark Parsons lives at 2201 Ninth Avenue, Tallahassee, Florida.

  b. Lisa bought twelve one-pound boxes of candy for the party.

  c. After 10 years of service, an employee may elect early retirement at age 55. The employer may also waive mandatory retirement at age sixty-five.

  d. The expert based his assumption on paragraph four on page 651.

  e. Last year, 12 corrections were made on pages 12-17 of the third printing.

  f. Check the figures in Chapter one, Column 3 of Figure 1.4.

5-10 Spell out a fraction when it occurs without a whole number. Hyphenate fractions immediately preceding a noun.

> Only about one half dozen of the members were present.
> Order one-half dozen ribbons.

■ Use figures to express a mixed number (a whole number and a fraction).

> Martha bought 4 1/2 boxes of potatoes.
> I need 1 1/4 rolls of red ribbon and 3 1/2 rolls of blue.

5-11 Spell out time when stated in numbers alone or before *o'clock*.

> I will meet you for coffee at eleven.
> The wedding will begin at six o'clock.

■ Use figures for time when *a.m.*, *noon*, and *p.m.* are used.

> Henrietta has a meeting at 10 a.m. and another at 2 p.m.
> The announcement will be made at 12 noon and 5 p.m.

5-6—5-9

a. C
b. **12** one-pound
c. After **ten** years
   age **fifty-five**
d. paragraph **4**
e. C
f. Chapter **1**

5-12 Use figures after a month to express the day and year. Set the year off by commas if the day directly precedes the year. Otherwise, do not use commas.

The events of November 21, 1975, will be long remembered.

The events of November 1975 will be long remembered.

■ Express the day in ordinal figures when the day precedes the month or the month is omitted. (In formal messages, ordinal words may be used.)

It was due on the 4th, but it's still not here.

He will arrive on the 2d of July and depart on the 3d.

Note: The preferred abbreviation of the ordinals *second* and *third* is *d* alone, not *nd* or *rd*.

This is the 103d day of the year.

  Proofread the following sentences for errors in the expression of numbers.

a. The pie-eating contest began at 12:01 p.m. on the 4th of August; the winner ate 6 1/2 pies.

b. Brody's sale will begin on June 20th at ten a.m.

c. Only one fourth of the participants will go on the first trip. The others will go within the next 2 weeks.

d. About 250 students are enrolled in evening classes; of them, nearly three fourths are employed full time.

e. Classes at Hopewell Community College begin at 8 o'clock in the morning and end at 5 o'clock in the afternoon.

f. It will be all right to give her an extension of sixty days beginning on May 3.

5-13 Use figures in expressing dimensions, measures, and weights.

The room was 9 by 12 feet in size.

The bucket of sand weighed 21 pounds.

The athlete was 6 feet 9 inches tall.

5-14 Use figures to express amounts of money. Decimals and zeroes are not used after even amounts unless they appear with fractional amounts.

Pauline earned $60 in tips.

Please pay $120.00 now and $61.50 for the next two months.

■ If the amount is less than a dollar, spell out the word *cents*.

There was an error of 25 cents on her statement.

■ In legal documents, express amounts of money or important figures in capitalized words followed by figures.

William Casady agrees to pay to the order of Sara Chambers Fifteen Hundred Dollars ($1,500) without interest.

5-15 Use figures to express percentages and decimals.

The loan was obtained at a rate of 9 percent.

Note: Spell out the word *percent* except in statistical material where the symbol (%) is used.

■ Use a zero before the decimal point for amounts less than one.

The accuracy percentage for all documents produced in the word processing center was 0.95, and 2,113 documents were produced.

5-16 Always use figures with abbreviations or symbols.

$9' \times 12'$ No. 345
$65°$ I-95

Proofread the following sentences for errors in the expression of numbers.

a. Enclosed is a check for $120.00 to guarantee the reservation for the 3d through the 5th of June.

b. The best rate that I could obtain on the mortgage was 10.5%.

c. Because of the absence of the person who introduced the bill, action on legislation relating to I-85 was postponed.

d. I was able to purchase the item for $18.99 at Brennan's, which is $.99 less than I would have paid for it at the hardware store.

e. Room 325 is $75 a day, but I can give you a 5 percent discount if you reserve it 14 days in advance.

f. A liter has about 1.8 ounces more than a quart.

Special Rules

This section provides special reminders concerning number usage. The importance of proofreading and correcting errors in number usage cannot be overemphasized. The proofreader must pay close attention to these reminders.

5-17 When a number consists of four or five figures, use commas to separate thousands, hundreds of thousands, etc.

5,000   320,267   43,824,321

Note: Do not, however, use commas when expressing years; page numbers; house, building, or room numbers; zip codes; telephone numbers; and decimal parts of numbers.

> page 1324
> 1584 Bayberry Drive, Cincinnati, OH 45230-8976
> (513) 323-1789
> 0.0125

5-18 Serial numbers are usually written without commas, but other marks of punctution and/or spaces are sometimes used.

> Invoice 38162
> Model G-4356
> Social Security No. 238-58-6600
> License No. 5014 587 035

5-13—5-16

a. **$120**
b. 10.5 **percent**
c. C
d. **99 cents**
e. C
f. C

5-19 Verify the accuracy of all numbers. Check all calculations.

The book was $3.50 and the card was 75 cents, making the total $4.35. (Cost is $4.25)

 Proofread the following sentences for statistical errors or errors in the expression of numbers.

a. The approved project will cost $365462, and it will be financed for 15 years at 12 percent.

b. Invoice No. 2,355 for $478.00 covers the cost of the range, Model C-3212.

c. Lynette's social security number is 237,66,0121, and her license number is 2021 21 365.

d. The cost of the small hammer is $5.95, which is 75 cents more than the larger $5.25 hammer.

e. The copyright year for stock number W02 is 1987.

f. Even with the $3000 grant, we are still $1200 short of covering our projected expenses.

Spelling Review

To improve your ability to detect spelling errors, master the words below. Watch for them in the exercises that follow and in succeeding chapters.

absence	fourth
accumulate	license
conscious	mortgage
copyright	ninth
extension	waive

5-17—5-19

a. $365,462
b. **2355 for $478**
c. 237-66-0121
d. **70** cents
e. C
f. $3,000 grant, we are still $1,200

Proofreading Tips

Study these tips and apply them as you proofread:

1. When possible, proofread numbers with another person, one reading the copy aloud, the other checking copy as it is read.

2. If numbers have been transferred from another document, verify that they have been copied correctly.

3. When figures are in columns, check that decimals are aligned.

4. Proofread columns of numbers across rather than down the columns. You will more easily detect omitted numbers.

5. Use a ruler or a straightedge to keep your place when proofreading numbers.

PROOFREADING APPLICATIONS

Proofread the following paragraphs and use the appropriate proofreading symbols to mark errors you find in expression of numbers and spelling. To aid you in proofreading, the number of errors to be found is indicated in parentheses at the end of Exercises P-1, P-2, and P-3. You must find them on your own in Exercise P-4.

P-1 The sellers are interested in marketing their three-bedroom, two-bath ranch home, which has just under sixteen hundred eighty square feet. The house, located at 5173 Nineth Street, is twenty-six years old, but the sellers have owned it for 12 years. Within the past two years, they have spent $3600 to repaint and install new neutral carpet. Room sizes are very livable, including a large country kitchen, which is 14 feet by 22 feet. The lot, which is just under 3/4 acre, is average for the neighborhood. (4)

P-2 To market their home, the sellers contacted a real estate company located just 3 blocks from their residence and made an appointment with an agent for 5 o'clock on Tuesday, February 15th. Upon meeting with the sellers, the agent pointed out that the real estate company was affiliated with a national relocation service and had consistently commanded 27 percent of the local market. Conscious of the value of experience, the agent also advised the sellers that she had had her lisence for five years. Furthermore, citing the 70 sales and listings she had accummulated over the past two years, the agent also demonstrated her personal success in marketing clients' homes. (5)

P-3 She warned the sellers of pitfalls that could occur should they wiave important inspections or accept an offer contingent upon the sale of another property. She provided the sellers with a comprehensive market analysis that reported similar homes in the neighborhood had sold in the previous three months for $62,500 to $65,000. Additionally, she discussed finance options. Considering the current 10.5 percent annual rate of interest, the agent felt that the home would be attractive to first-time

P-1

1. **1,680** square feet
2. 5173 **Ninth** Street
3. $3,600
4. **three-fourths**

P-2

1. **three** blocks
2. **five** o'clock
3. February **15**
4. **license**
5. **accumulated**

buyers. If the home sold for $64,000, the typical buyer could obtain a 90% morgage, and the PITI (principal, interest, taxes and insurance) would cost just over $625.00 monthly. Finally, conscience of the psychology used by retailers in pricing items at $.99 instead of $1.00, the agent advised the sellers to list their home at $65,499. (7)

P-4   "The Value of Investing in Heating Efficiency" on page 73 of the March/April 1986 issue of *Real Estate Today* shows the returns a homeowner could expect if he or she invested in energy conservation measures. According to the article, average heating bills for a house with fifteen hundred square feet and 4 occupants situated in a climate where temperatures range between 90° and − 10° are $1600 per year. With an investment to save energy, it would be possible to accrue a net savings of more than $45,000.00 over the life of the loan (assuming an annual 6% increase in fuel prices).

P-3

1. waive
2. 90 **percent**
3. mortgage
4. **$625** monthly
5. **conscious**
6. **99 cents**
7. $1

P-4

1. **1,500** square feet
2. **four** occupants
3. **$1,600**
4. **$45,000**
5. 6 **percent**

PROGRESSIVE PROOFREADING

The following section provides an opportunity for you to apply your proofreading skills to a job situation:

You are employed as office manager for the Phelps Real Estate Agency. The agency uses the block letter style with open punctuation. One of your responsibilities is that of proofreading all of the documents produced by the other four office employees. In your basket today are three items to be proofread.

Job 1: An article written by Tom Phelps, the owner of a local real estate publication.

Job 2: Minutes of the monthly meeting of the Delhi Association of Realtors.

Job 3: A letter to a client.

Job 1 Proofread the following article.

SHOULD YOU USE A REAL ESTATE AGENT?

Do you need a real estate agent when you buy or sell a house? Your immediate response might be that enlisting the help of a professional would be unnecessary. However, unless you have plenty of time and lots of experience, you could be taking a large risk if you do not seek the help of a professional realtor.

An agent can provide buyers with pertinent information to help them meet their location needs. The requirements of a family with a 10-year old child will be different from those of a couple with grown children. The proximity of a good school and recreational facilities is important to parents with young children.

A professional agent can also advise a buyer on an affordable price range based on yearly income. For example, should a buyer with an income of $35,000 be looking at homes in the $90,000 range? An experienced agent would advise the buyer to spend no more than two and one half times gross income. Debt factors, however, must also be considered.

Once the buyer has found a suitable house, the agent can guide the buyer through the transaction by helping to negotiate a price and by putting the buyer in touch with morgage lenders, contractors, appraisers, inspectors, and insurance agents.

A professional realtor can also save a seller time, money, and frustration. Too often a homeonwer seeks the help of a professional only after having incurred problems. One seller spent $350 on advertising, $300 on travel showing the house, $78.25 on phone calls,

CHAPTER 5—Proofreading for Errors in Expression of Numbers

and $800 on maintainence while the house was on the market (a to-
tal of $1,438.25. Additionally, the client suffered a great deal
of frustration before engaging a professional realtor.

When enlisting the help of a real estate agent, keep the following points in mind:

1. Ask for references from clients who have bought property
recently.

2. Investigate the community in which you are interested.

4. Deal with a professional agent "who has a good reputation"

5. Find out if the company which the realtor represents
belongs to the local real estate board.

By taking advantage of an agent's experience, access to properties, and information about the local real estate market, people
can avoid the pitfalls inherent in purchasing or marketing thier
homes.

Delhi Association of Realtors
325 Alabama Street
Indianapolis, IN 46204-6154
(317) 555-7355

MINUTES OF MEETING
DELHI ASSOCIATION OF REALTORS

Place of
Meeting

The Delhi Assoc. of Realtors held its monthly meeting
on Tuesday, January 18, 19--, at The Heritage Restaurant. The social hour began at 6:00 o'clock, and dinner
was served at 7. Seventy-eight of the 85 members were
present in addition to four guests.

Call to
Order

Immediately following dinner, J.R. Hawkins, president,
called the meeting to order and welcomed the members
and guests. She noted that the January attendance was
10% above the December attendance.

Approval of
Minutes

The minutes were presented by Secretary Tom Phelps.
Jim Miller noted that the state convention would be
held on the nineth of March instead of on April 10 as
stated in the minutes. The correction was made, and
the minutes were approved.

Treasurer's
Report

In the absense of Susan Peoples, Tom Phelps gave the
treasurer's report. The Association has a balance of
$1,210 in the treasury, and bills amounting to $75.10
($35.10 to Rouse Printing Company and $41 to The Heritage Restaurant) are outstanding. An extention of 10
days has been granted to members who haven't paid their
dues.

Market
Review

Robert Blakenship was called upon to give a summary
of the developments that have taken place in the local
real estate market. Phelps Real Estate Company has
been selected as exclusive marketing agent for Breckenridge subdivision on Leesville Rd. The 79-lot single-
family subdivision is a Drexter development. Northwoods
Village, a 228-unit luxury apartment community developed
by Dallas C. Pickford & Associates, will open on the
1st of August. The community is located at Ten Northwood
Village Drive, one-half mile south of Interstate 40.

Speaker

Following the business session, the president introduced
Mrs. Sarah Dunbarton, president of Dunbarton Associates,
as speaker for the meeting. Mrs. Dunbarton discussed
the potential effects of recent tax legislation on the
real estate market. She predicted that the prime rate
will drop another half point before it hits bottom. In
In the local area, there will probably be an increase
of 12-15 apartment buildings on the market within the
next 6 months.

Adjournment   Following the presentation, the treasurer drew the
               lucky number to determine who would win the center-
               piece. 320 was the lucky number, and winner was Joann
               Durham.

               The meeting was adjourned at 9:15 p.m. Members were
               reminded that the next meeting would be on the third
               Tuesday of February.

                              Respectfully submitted,

                              Tom Phelps, Secretary

Job 3 Proofread the letter below.

Phelps Real Estate Agency

1125 Umstead Drive   Indianapolis, IN   46204-6154   (317) 555-3222

August 19, 19--

Ms. Patricia Strum
1 Kildaire Farm Road
Indianapolis, IN   46205-9241

Dear Ms. Strum

I have some good news for you! The house you are interested in on thirty-third Street has been reduced $5,000. The price is now within the range you mentioned to me on the forth. May I urge you to act quickly.

Because of the favorable mortgage interest rates that are now a-vailable, you can own this 2200-square-foot house and still have mortgage payments of less than $900 per month. For a limited time, the Indianapoles Federal Savings and Loan Association will approve your application for an adjustable rate loan within 30 days. If it is not approved, you will not be charged the 1% discount rate.

Please call me at 555-3222 to set up an appointment. My office hours are from 9:00 to 5 p.m. during the week.

Sincerely

Terry B. Andrus
Agent

df

Chapter 6

Proofreading for Errors in Format

Objectives: *After completing this chapter, you should be able to*

1. Recognize format errors in letters, envelopes, interoffice memorandums, and reports.
2. Use appropriate proofreading symbols to indicate changes in text.
3. Apply helpful tips when proofreading for format errors.

Importance of Formats

A favorable first impression of any business document is important. Why? Because the reader forms an opinion—favorable or unfavorable—of the writer and the message based upon the appearance of the document. The overall appearance is affected by the neatness of the document, the quality of the print and stationery, and the format of the document.

Format is perhaps the most complex factor in the appearance of a business document. The format of a document includes its margin settings, its vertical spacing, and the placement of its various parts. If the document is produced on a printer, the format may also include the use of various print sizes (or pitches) and print styles (such as boldface or italic).

The proper use of format is essential to the production of quality copy. Incorrect use of format can destroy the credibility of a document instantly. Chapter 6 will provide a review and application of the basic rules that govern the standard formats of letters, interoffice memorandums, and reports. To be a good proofreader, you must be very knowledgeable of these rules and apply them consistently. (Note: Solutions for the exercises in Chapter 6 begin on page 218.)

6-1 The proofreading symbols that apply to formatting are shown below.

_SS_ Single-space.

_SS_ Ms. Jane P. Fore
1237 Pine Lane

_DS_ Double-space.

_DS_ Dear Mr. Sebastian
We have recalled your radio.

_TS_ Triple-space.

_TS_ Subject: Work Summary
Unit 10 completed five projects.

_QS_ Quadruple-space.

_QS_ Sincerely yours,
Walter Post

_¶_ Start a new paragraph.

He ended his story. _¶_ Martha rose
to begin. . .

_↰_ Move copy as indicated.

Second, fertilize the plant on a
bimonthly basis. First, check to
be sure the plant is receiving
adequate light and water.

_||_ Align copy.

||1. To improve skill in arranging...
  2. To improve spelling...

_lc or /_ Change to lowercase.

_lc_ MARTIN Henry introduced Himself.

Cap or ≡ Change to a capital letter.

cap 2121 barker street

ital. or ___ Italicize a word or phrase.

ital He reported on an article in The Wall
Street Journal.

_⊓ ⊔_ Raise copy; lower copy.

The importance of getting into...
The survey indicates a need for
teachers.

_⊐ ⊏_ Move right; move left.

Terry Jones
1910 Spring Street
Oxford, OH 45056-9321

Dear Terry

_no ¶_ Do not start a new paragraph.

The two girls were hired the same day.
_no ¶_ They became acquainted and...

_____ Change copy as noted.

Miss Diaz
Dear Madam

Review these marks carefully, and note how they are used in the rough
draft shown on page 67. Then note the changes that have been made in the
finished letter.

Rough Draft

Finished Letter

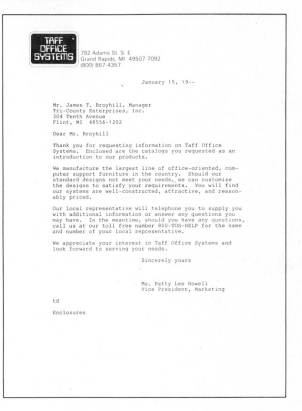

 Did the typist make all of the necessary changes?_____

Letter Format

Locating format errors in business letters requires that the proofreader be familiar with the correct sequence and placement of letter parts. Refer to Illustration 6-1 on page 68 as you review each of the letter parts. Placement of the letter parts and punctuation may vary with the style of letter used. These specific points will be discussed in the subsequent section on letter styles.

Date

To allow space for the company letterhead, the date should be placed between two and three inches from the top of the page, depending upon the length of the letter. Many businesses, however, use a standard or set placement for the date regardless of the letter length. A common standard placement is line 15. When using either convention, allow at least a double space between the last line of the letterhead and the date.

Illustration 6-1   Correctly formatted letter

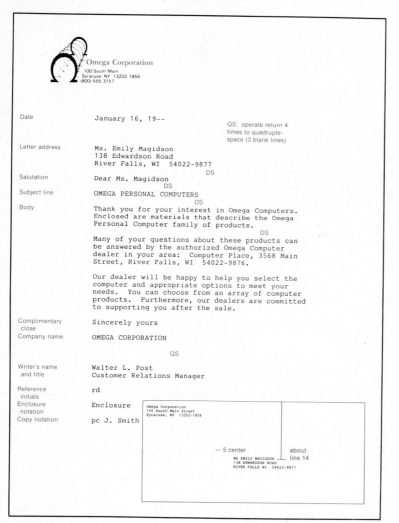

If the letter is prepared on plain stationery rather than on company letter-head, the writer's return address should be placed immediately above the date.

Letter Address

The letter address gives complete information about the person to whom the letter is directed. It should contain the recipient's name, title (when appropriate), and complete address. If the letter is addressed to a company, an attention line may be included as the second line of the letter address. The letter address should begin on the fourth line (3 blank lines) below the date. The proofreader should always check spellings of the name, street, and city to be sure they are correct.

If the addressee is an individual, a personal title (Mr., Miss, Ms., Dr., etc.) should precede the name. If the letter is addressed to a woman whose personal title is not known, use "Ms." Official titles (Chairman, Vice President of Operations) in the letter address should be capitalized.

Note: The address on the envelope should agree with the letter address. Refer to Illustration 6-1 for proper envelope format.

Salutation

The salutation (greeting) used must agree with the first line of the letter address. The salutation is placed a double space below the letter address. The examples below show the proper salutations to be used in different situations. Note that only the first word, nouns, and titles are capitalized in a formal salutation.

Addressed to a company:	Melvin & Watson 1592 Collinsdale Cincinnati, OH 45230-6590 DS Ladies and Gentlemen
Addressed to a job title:	Advertising Manager Melvin & Watson 1592 Collinsdale Cincinnati, OH 45230-6590 DS Dear Sir or Madam
Addressed to an individual:	Mrs. Ruby B. Speight 1500 Sauls Street Covington, KY 41011-9750 DS My dear Mrs. Speight

Subject Line

The subject line, which indicates the topic of the letter, is placed a double space below the salutation. The subject line is usually keyed in ALL CAPS at the left margin, but it may be centered or aligned with the first word of paragraph 1, depending on the format style used.

Body

The body, or message, begins a double space below the salutation or subject line. The body is single spaced with a double space between paragraphs.

Complimentary Close

The complimentary close provides a cordial farewell. It should be placed a double space below the body of the letter. Only the first word of a complimentary close is capitalized.

Company Name and Writer's Name and Title

When letterhead stationery is used, the company name is rarely included in the closing lines. If the company name is used, it should be placed a double space below the complimentary close in ALL CAPS .

The sender's name should be entered on the fourth line (3 blank lines) below the complimentary close (or the company name if it is included). The use of the personal title in the closing lines is preferred so that others may address correspondence correctly. The sender's official title may be placed on the same line as the typed signature and separated from the signature by a comma or may be placed on the next line. The individual's title should be capitalized.

Reference Initials

Reference initials identify those involved in the creation of a business letter. These initials should be located at the left margin, a double space below the signer's typed name and title.

Enclosure Notation

The enclosure notation is used when one or more documents accompany the letter. For the notation, the word *Enclosure* or *Enclosures* is spelled out in full. The notation should be placed at the left margin, a double space below the reference initials.

Copy Notation

The copy notation indicates other persons who will receive a copy of the letter. The copy notation appears in lowercase at the left margin as "cc"(carbon copy), "pc" (photocopy), or "bc" (blind copy). The blind copy notation is used when the originator does not want the addressee to know that a certain individual is receiving a copy; it does not appear on the addressee's copy. The copy notation should be placed a double space below the reference initials or below the enclosure notation if there is one.

6-2 When proofreading a business letter, make sure all appropriate letter parts are included, properly typed, and positioned.

Proofread the following letter parts for format errors, using appropriate proofreading symbols to mark errors. Refer to page 218 for the solutions.

a. Ms. Katrina Ann Dewar
    8577 Estate Drive South
    West Palm Beach, FL 33411-9753

    Sales Promotion

    Dear Madam

b. Please let me know when we can get together to discuss the
    property.

    Very Sincerely Yours,

    Ms. Donna Raynor

    Enclosure

    ah

c. Carson Real Estate Enterprises
    1860 Memorial Drive
    Greenville, SC 29605-8642

    Dear Mr. Carson

d. Mr. M. C. Alexander
    1620 Quantico Court
    San Jose, CA 95230-1009

    Dear Mr. M. C. Alexander

e. Ms. Ilo Carlson
    8090 Pinetree Street
    Little Rock, AR 72201-0057

    My Dear Mrs. Carlson

f. Sincerely,

    Brian Davis, Manager
    dt
    cc Carolyn Walston

Letter and Punctuation Styles

As mentioned in the previous section, punctuation and placement of some letter parts vary with the style selected. The following paragraphs describe the various letter and punctuation styles that may be used in letter preparation.

Although various letter styles are acceptable, the most popular are the block style and the modified block style. Usually organizations prepare all of their correspondence using the same style. Refer to Illustration 6-2 below for a review of the block and modified block letter styles. Paragraphs may be either blocked (begun at the left margin) or indented in the modified block style.

Letters may be prepared using either open or mixed punctuation. Open punctuation includes no punctuation after the salutation or the complimentary close. Mixed punctuation includes a colon after the salutation and a comma after the complimentary close.

Illustration 6-2   **Block Style**   **Modified Block Style**

6-3 Remember to use the correct format consistently, regardless of the letter style chosen.

Proofread the letter shown below and mark the errors using appropriate proofeading symbols. Pay attention to the letter style, placement of letter parts, and punctuation style. The letter should be prepared in block style with open punctuation. Then compare your work with the solution given on page 218.

WALSH PAPERS

2250 Harris Road
Huntsville, AL 35810-2250
(509) 555-5892

June 16, 19--

Ms. Jennifer Elaine Carson
Route 2, Box 507B
Huntsville, AL 35807-8615

PURCHASE ORDER 471

My Dear Ms. Carson

Thank you for your order for six boxes of stationery, Stock No. 331. The quality of the stationery you have selected will let your customers know that they are important to you.

Because of the recent shipping strike, there has been a delay in our receiving the merchandise from the factory. We have been informed that the shipment has been sent, however, and we should receive it within a week. Your order will be on its way to you as soon as we receive the shipment. We hope this delay will not inconvenience you too much.

We appreciate the business you have given us in the past, and we look forward to serving you in the future.

Sincerely,

Audrey D. Leapley, Manager
Shipping Department

ec
pc R. P. Michaels

Letter Placement

The spacing and placement of the various letter parts contribute to the readability of a document, as well as to its overall attractiveness. Placing a letter too high or too low on the paper or too far to the left or the right upsets the balance and detracts from the letter's appearance. In order for a letter to have an attractive overall appearance, the typist must use appropriate side, top, and bottom margins. These margins depend upon the size of stationery used (standard size, executive size, and half-size) and the length of the letter to be typed.

As a proofreader, you should be more concerned with the overall balance of a letter than with its exact margins. Regardless of the size of the stationery and the length of the document, the letter should appear "framed" on the page. Your goal in proofreading will be to train your eye to identify an improperly placed letter.

6-4   Begin now to develop good judgment concerning letter placement by making a conscious appraisal of the placement of every letter you see.

 Study the three letters given and indicate which letter is properly placed.

Letter A   Letter B   Letter C

The correct placement is shown in Letter _____.

Memorandum Format

Interoffice memorandums are used to send informal messages within an organization. Memorandums cover one subject or topic that can be discussed in a few paragraphs. Even though the interoffice memorandum is for internal use, accuracy of the message and the proper format are still important. Coworkers and managers often judge the writer's overall job abilities by the quality of the message the writer sends. Additionally, improper format tends to distract the reader.

Printed interoffice memorandum forms are used by a majority of business firms. The forms usually have four main headings: TO, FROM, DATE and SUBJECT. Headings appear in all capitals. If the organization does not use a form with printed headings, headings should be positioned so that the same margin setting can be used to fill in the headings and to enter the body. Side margins are usually 1 inch, and the message is single spaced with a double space between paragraphs. The message should begin a triple space below the last heading. Memos are usually signed or initialed by the originator. Study the illustration below so that you will be able to proofread interoffice memos quickly and effectively.

Illustration 6-3   Interoffice Memorandum

KRIEGER PHARMACEUTICALS

Internal Memorandum

TO: All Employees

FROM: Pat Brooks, Personnel Manager *PB*

DATE: May 20, 19--

SUBJECT: Vacation Policies

TS

The new vacation policy issued last week will be implemented beginning June 1. Please submit your request for vacation time as soon as you can so that we can try to accommodate your preferences.

Plan to take the full vacation to which you are entitled. Studies show that taking only a day or two of vacation at a time does not maximize the benefits to you of time taken off from work.

lj

6-5   Apply the guidelines above when proofreading memorandums.

Proofread the following interoffice memorandum for errors in format, using the appropriate proofreading symbols. Check your solution on page 219.

Martindale Publishing   **Internal Memorandum**

TO: Associate Editors

FROM: Danny Bright, Executive Editor

DATE: Production Meetings

SUBJECT: April 10, 19--

      On Monday, April 25, all associate editors should plan to
meet in Conference Room C, third floor, at 10 a.m.   The purpose
of this meeting is to identify topics which are of concern to
you as a supervisor.
      You are a vital member of our editorial team, and your input
is essential to keeping production running smoothly during this
very heavy copyright year. Based on your input, we will establish
an agenda for future meetings.

      re

Report Format

Reports are used extensively by business and educational institutions to provide information on specific topics. Standard parts of a report include the title page, main heading, body, side headings, paragraph headings, and reference page. Reports may be long, formal documents consisting of a number of parts; or they may be short, informal documents consisting of only a heading and the body of the report.

Reports may be prepared in unbound, leftbound, or topbound format. Most reports, however, are prepared in unbound format and are simply held together by a staple at the top.

Just as with business letters and memorandums, reports should be positioned in an attractive, easy-to-read format. Refer to the model report on page 78 as you review the format for the main parts of a report.

Title Page

The title page contains the name of the report, the author, the name of the class (if applicable), and the date. Refer to the example title page on page 78.

Margins

In unbound report format, 1-inch margins are used for the side and bottom margins. A top margin of about 2 inches is used for the first page. On the second and succeeding pages, a top margin of 1 inch is used, with the page number on line 4 and the text continuing on line 7.

In leftbound report format, the left margin should be 1 1/2 inches to allow space for the binding. All other margins are the same as for an unbound report.

Headings

The *main heading* should be centered about 2 inches from the top of the page and should be entered in ALL CAPS. If two lines are required, the lines may be either single spaced or double spaced.

Side headings indicate subdivisions of the main topic. Side headings should be entered in capital and lowercase letters (important words capitalized) and underlined. A triple space should precede a side heading and a double space should follow it.

Paragraph headings indicate subdivisions of the side headings. Paragraph headings should be indented five spaces from the left margin. The first word is capitalized, and the heading is underlined and followed with a period. The text of the paragraph should begin on the same line as the heading.

Body

The body or the text of a report should begin a triple space (two blank lines) below the main heading. The paragraphs are usually indented and double spaced, with a double space between the paragraphs. Some companies prefer long reports be single spaced. In this case, a double space is used between paragraphs.

Page Numbers

The first page of a report usually is not numbered. On the second page and subsequent pages, the page number should be placed on line 4 at the right margin. The body of the report continues on line 7.

Illustration 6-4   **Model Report**

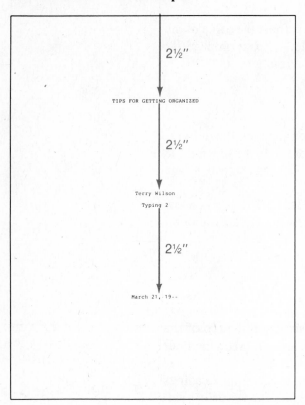

2½″

TIPS FOR GETTING ORGANIZED

2½″

Terry Wilson

Typing 2

2½″

March 21, 19--

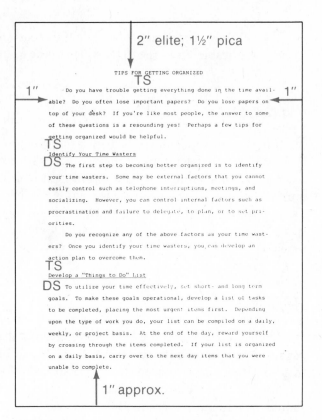

2″ elite; 1½″ pica

TIPS FOR GETTING ORGANIZED

TS

1″   Do you have trouble getting everything done in the time available? Do you often lose important papers? Do you lose papers on   1″
top of your desk? If you're like most people, the answer to some
of these questions is a resounding yes! Perhaps a few tips for
getting organized would be helpful.

TS

Identify Your Time Wasters

DS   The first step to becoming better organized is to identify
your time wasters. Some may be external factors that you cannot
easily control such as telephone interruptions, meetings, and
socializing. However, you can control internal factors such as
procrastination and failure to delegate, to plan, or to set pri-
orities.

    Do you recognize any of the above factors as your time wast-
ers? Once you identify your time wasters, you can develop an
action plan to overcome them.

TS

Develop a "Things to Do" List

DS   To utilize your time effectively, set short- and long-term
goals. To make these goals operational, develop a list of tasks
to be completed, placing the most urgent items first. Depending
upon the type of work you do, your list can be compiled on a daily,
weekly, or project basis. At the end of the day, reward yourself
by crossing through the items completed. If your list is organized
on a daily basis, carry over to the next day items that you were
unable to complete.

1″ approx.

1″   Line 4 ₂

    Develop your "Things to Do" list daily at a time that is best
for you. This list may be completed while riding the bus to work
in the morning or may be done during the last ten minutes of the
previous work day.

Maintain a Recording and Filing System

    To eliminate countless frustrations and to save time search-
ing for items, keep pertinent information in an accessible place.
Two such places are a pocket organizer and your personal files.

    Pocket organizer. Carry a pocket organizer to record appoint-
ments, expenses, addresses and telephone numbers, reminders, and
jobs to be done. Such an organizer will become a valuable tool.

    Filing system. Locating important papers is easier if you
only have to look in one place--your files. Label folders appropriately; for example, automobile, credit card statements, health,
household, medical, property, taxes, travel, and warranties.

Handle Paperwork Once

    Handle each piece of paperwork once--do it, dump it, or dele-
gate it. If paperwork must be delayed, set a deadline for completion. When you delegate, be sure to set a deadline for return.
If you think something may be useful some day, throw it out; it's
probable that you won't need it.

Conclusion

    Time is a valuable resource that few people have enough of.
The aim of time management (Kelling and Kallus, 1983) is to provide
for efficient use of resources, including time, so that individuals
are productive in achieving . . . their goals.

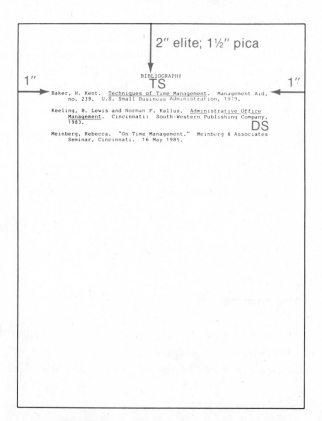

2″ elite; 1½″ pica

BIBLIOGRAPHY

TS

1″   Baker, H. Kent. Techniques of Time Management. Management Aid,   1″
    no. 239. U.S. Small Business Administration, 1979.

Keeling, B. Lewis and Norman F. Kallus. Administrative Office
    Management. Cincinnati: South-Western Publishing Company,
    1983.   DS

Meinberg, Rebecca. "On Time Management." Meinberg & Associates
    Seminar, Cincinnati. 16 May 1985.

References

When quoting another writer or when using another's ideas, writers must document (identify) their source(s). A common method of documentation is to cite the source of the information within the body of the report. This reference includes the author's last name, the year of publication, and the page number.

According to Macey (1985, 74)

Complete information about the sources is found on the bibliography page, a list of references at the end of the report. Each entry on the page consists of the name(s) of the author(s), the title and date of the referenced publication, and the page number(s) of the material cited. Refer to page 78 for an example of a bibliography page.

6-6 Follow these tips whenever you are proofreading a report, especially a long report.

■ Develop a style sheet or a list showing how unusual terminology, features, punctuation, capitalization, names, or titles will be handled. Using a style sheet will help you to treat items consistently.

■ If the report has been prepared from a draft copy, check to be sure that copy has not been omitted in typing.

■ If the text refers to a particular illustration, figure, or page within the report, check to be sure the reference is correct.

■ If you are responsible for checking the references given in the report, look each one up to verify it.

■ As a final check, proofread separately similar parts of a lengthy report. For example, check all the side headings to see if they are handled consistently; then check all the paragraph headings. Also, check that all pages have been numbered in sequence.

Refer to the Progressive Proofreading section for an opportunity to exercise your skills in proofreading reports.

Spelling Review

To improve your ability to detect spelling errors, master the words below. Watch for them in the exercises that follow and in succeeding chapters.

column	particularly
description	precede
eliminate	separate
judgment	sufficient
opportunity	usable

Proofreading Tips

Study these tips and apply them as you proofread:

1. Watch for the places where errors tend to occur: in words located near the margins; in lines close to the bottom of the page; in long words; in titles, headings, and subheadings.

2. Use an up-to-date reference guide. (Because of increased use of the personal computer, some format rules may change.)

3. Don't overlook proofreading the date, letter address, salutation, and closing lines within a letter.

4. Be sure the format of the letter is not a mixture of block and modified block or that the punctuation styles are not mixed.

5. When completing a large mailing, make sure letters are put in the proper envelopes and all enclosures are included.

PROGRESSIVE PROOFREADING

The following section provides an opportunity for you to apply your proofreading skills to a job situation:

You are employed as executive secretary to Ms. Emily Simpson, regional manager of Perin Office Systems, Inc. You have just finished typing three documents that she dictated. In addition to proofreading them, you need to proofread the documents prepared by a typist who works with you. Check for errors in typing, spelling, word division, number expression, and format.

Jobs 1-3: Proofread the letter to Mr. Gardner (Job 1) and the letter and report (Jobs 2 and 3) being sent to Eastman Brothers, Inc.

Jobs 4-5: Proofread the two documents (Jobs 4-5) for the typist, following the instructions left for you.

Job 1 Proofread the letter to Mr. Gardner. Ms. Simpson prefers the block letter style and open punctuation.

PERIN OFFICE SYSTEMS
3903 Spaulding Drive
Atlanta, GA 30338-3903
(404) 555-1719

March 17, 19--

Mr. Lloyd Gardner
Vocational Education Director
Tallahassee City Schools
Tallahassee, FL 32308-5489

Dear Ms. Gardner:

Thank you for the opportunity to demonstrate our equipment to the office education teachers again this year at
the Tallahase Vocational Drive-In Conference on May 16.
Yes, we would be delighted to exhibit.

We think teachers should be particulary interested in the
Perin electronic typewriters and our new high-speed desk-
top copier. We also plan to exhibit the Perin II Personal
Computer and a variety of peripherals.

Your description of the exhibit area and available space
inidates to me that we would be exhibiting in a prime
location, and your charges for this location are equitable. Because we are interested in getting maximum
exposure, we are willing to pay the top price. We appreciate your opening the exhibits 1 hour preceeding the
first session.

Sincerely yours

Ms. Emily E. Simpson
Regional Manager

mr

Job 2 Letter to Eastman Brothers.

PERIN OFFICE SYSTEMS
3903 Spaulding Drive
Atlanta, GA 30338-3903
(404) 555-1719

March 17, 19--

Mr. Roger Moe
Eastman Brothers, Inc.
7861 Monroe Street
Tallahassee, FL 32301-7654

Ladies and Gentlemen

Enclosed is a short report reviewing the preliminary
design factors that your project committee must consider
when planning the 15,000-square-foot addition to your
existing facilities.

We will provide complete documentation for these reccomen-
dations atour initial planning session on Apirl 7. In
the mean time, good luck with your planning.

Sincerely yours,

Ms. Emily E. Simpson
Regional Manager

jp

Enclosure

Job 3 Report to Eastman Brothers.

OFFICE DESIGN FACTORS

Eastman Brothers, Inc.

Because office design does affect job performance and job satis faction, several factors should be considered in the preliminary
stages of planning the construction or renovation of any facility.
This report discusses these factors and gives recommendations which
may increase employees' productivity by as much as 30% and decrease a-
bsenteeism.

Work Space

The area where workers spend most of their time is their work
space. The factors to be considered when work space is designed
are discussed below.

Enclosures. The open-office plan with enclosures gives workers the privacy they need, supports communication, and improves
productivity more than either the fully open or fully closed
office plans. To be effective, the partitions surrounding each work
area should be higher than standing height on 3 sides

Floor area. The amount of usable flour space a worker can call
his or her own is based on job need and status. According to recent research (Brill 1985), the minimum requirements for various
workers are as follows:

Managers	115 square feet
Professional/technical workers	82 square feet
Clerical worders	43 square feet

Layout. The physical arrangement (layout) of furniture and walls greatly affects job performance, comfort, status, and ease of communication. Workers should have two good work surfaces and a single front entrance. The layout should be designed so that others are not seated directly in front of the employee.

Lighting.

Proper lighting is determined by the quality and quantity of light. The quantity and quality of light affects proper lighting. Approxmately 150 fc (footcandles) are recommended for computer usage. Most lightning problems are caused by too much light resulting in in glare on documents or reflections on monitors. Although most workers prefer to be near a window, windows do cause glare.

Ambient light fixtures (which illuminate the entire office area) combined with task lighting (which lights specific work surfaces) create the most effective lighting system.

Noise

Office conversations, ringing telephones, and outside nose account for most office noise. Sound-absorbent materials used throughout the building, acoustical enclosures on printers, and layout are effective means of reducing office noise. Office noise should be less then 65 decibels (Casady 1984).

Energy

Energy needs include lines for power, phones, and data. Questions to be answered in determining energy needs are (1) Do you expect high growth in computer usage? and (2) Do you expect to rearrange workstations frequently? how often?

Access floors raised of the structural slab provide an excellent solution for distributing heat, air conditioning, and wiring for data and telephone services. These floors have un-limited capacity and may be accessed at any point by service units without calling an electrician. Additionally, quality and speed of transmission will not be affected as your transmission needs grwo.

Job 4 Compare the typed letter on the following page to the rough draft below. Mr. Holms prefers the modified block style and mixed punctuation.

Send this letter to Jessica Shimer, 2905 Sandcastle Dr.,
Tallahassee 32308-9625

Thank you for your interest in the Perin Laser Copier, Model

212. Enclosed is a brochure detailing its unique features, its

specifications., *and its cost*.

Perin's Laser Copier is the most techn~o~logically sophisticated

copier on the market today. ∧~Perin's Laser Copier is actually~

~two seperate units: a digital scanner and a laser printer.~

Because it is digital, the laser copier can transmit images to

other printers and produce high-resolution copies in seconds.

After you have had a chance to review this brochure, I will

give you a call to provide you with additional product or price

info or to set up a demonstration for you. In the mean time,

please call me at the number listed above if you have any questions.

Sincerely yours--Robert C. Holms, Sales Rep.

*This laser-driven copier uses a scanner
to digitize ∧paper originals. ~Additional~ text (including
colums) can be manipulated before printing
begins.*

Enclosure

PERIN OFFICE SYSTEMS

3903 Spaulding Drive
Atlanta, GA 30338-3903
(404) 555-1719

March 17, 19--

Jessica Shimer
2905 Sandcastle Dr.
Tallahassee, FL 32308-9625

Dear Ms. Shimer:

Thank you for your interest in the Perin Laser Copier,
Model 212. Enclosed is a brochure detailing its unique
features, its specifications, and its cost.

Perin's Laser Copier is the most technologically sophisticated copier on the marked today. This laser-driven
copier uses a scanner to digitize originals. Text (including columns can be manipulated before printing them.
Because it is digital, the laser copier can transmit
images to other printers and produce high-resolution
copiers in seconds.

After you have had a chance to review this brochure, I
will give you a call to provide you with additional product or price information or to set up a demonstration.
In the meantime, please call me at the number listed
above if you have any questions.

Sincerely yours,

Robert C. Holms
Saels Representative

tr

Job 5 Proofread the memorandum transcribed from dictation.

PERIN OFFICE SYSTEMS

Internal Memorandum

TO: All Product Managers

FROM: Larry Bryant, Systems Manager

DATE: March 17, 19--

SUBJECT: Computer Maintenence

As more and more managers are accessing computer terminals or are acquiring their own, it becomes increasingly important that everyone practice good procedures for operating and maintaining computer terminals and peripherals. Please review these procedures to keep your equipment in good working order.

1. Keep your equipment away from direct sunlight, heat vents, and open windows. Extreme temperatures can damage chips and other components.

2. Keep food and beverages away from equipment and diskettes.

3. Eliminate smoking near equipment. Tobacco smoke contains dust and tars that can damage or clog equipment.

4. Keep paper clips that have been stored in a magnetic container away from diskettes. Keep diskettes away from magents or any electronic equipment. These items contain magnetic fields that can cause portions of text to be erased.

4. Use anti static mats under your computer. Static electricity can cause memory loss.

5. Never oil your printer or any part of your system. Oil will clog the machine.

6. Check power requirements to be sure your power is sufficent.

7. Do not take anything apart, even if in your judgment you can fix it. Call Helen Mathys (Ext. 278), and she will contact our service representative.

tr

Chapter 7

Proofreading for Grammatical Errors, Part 1

Objectives: *After completing this chapter, you should be able to*

1. Recognize sentence fragments.
2. Identify errors in subject-verb agreement.
3. Identify misplaced and dangling modifiers.
4. Use appropriate proofreading symbols to indicate changes in text.

Importance of Correct Grammar

The proofreader must be alert for grammatical errors. In addition to clarifying the message, correct grammar conveys a message to the reader about the writer. It reflects the writer's abilities and attention to detail. The reader will have greater confidence in the writer if the message is grammatically correct. If it is not correct, the reader will react negatively and lose confidence in the writer or the person or company the writer represents. This chapter will review the rules concerning basic sentence structure, subject-verb agreement, and placement of modifiers. Because grammar is essential to effective communication, study carefully the rules reviewed here and in Chapter 8.

Parts of a Sentence

A sentence is a group of words that expresses a complete thought. It requires both a subject and a verb. The **subject** is the person, place, or thing spoken of in the sentence, and the **verb** indicates what the subject is or does. The verb expresses action (*eat, sleep, think*) or a state of being (*is, am, are, seem*).

7-1 An incomplete sentence, termed a *sentence fragment*, does not contain both a subject and a verb and does not express a complete thought. Rewrite sentence fragments to change them into complete sentences.

Sentence Fragment: Promoted the clerk and hired a replacement.

Complete Sentence: Martha promoted the clerk and hired a replacement.

Identify each of the following groups of words as either a sentence or a fragment by writing *S* or *F* after each group. Correct sentence fragments by adding words to make complete sentences.

a. Your order of January 29 has been filled.

b. A number of out-of-date items in the files.

c. A price list and an order blank are enclosed.

d. Her contract has been extended for two years.

e. Reads and writes well for a third grader.

7-2   The subject of a sentence is usually a noun (Barbara, New York, hat) or a personal pronoun (*I, you, he, she, it, we, they*). A **pronoun** is a word used in place of a noun.

<pre>
        S   V
Dr. Morgan signed the contract.
      (noun used as a subject)

    S   V
He signed the contract.
  (pronoun used as a subject)
</pre>

Indicate whether the subject of each sentence is a noun or a pronoun by writing either *N* or *P* above the subject.

a. Ms. Chandler presided at the meeting.

b. He was elected secretary of the committee.

c. You have a lot of natural talent.

d. Sean taught his brother to use the software.

e. They saluted the flag as it passed.

Subject-Verb Agreement

The verb must agree with its subject in number. Rules on subject-verb agreement are given in the frames that follow.

7-1

a. S

b. items~in the files.   *are*

c. S

d. S

e. Reads and writes well   *Jordan*

   for a third grader.

7-3   A singular subject must have a singular verb, and a plural subject must have a plural verb.

$$\overset{S}{\text{The author}}\ \overset{V}{\text{writes}}\ \text{clearly.}$$

The author writes clearly.

The two books appear to be lost.

- The personal pronouns *I*, *he*, *she*, and *it* require a singular verb; *you*, *we*, and *they* require a plural verb. *You* always requires a plural verb even when it is used in the singular sense.

I am going to exercise daily.

We are going to jog weekly.

You know the limitations of the program.

You and Pat know the limitations of the program.

She writes very concisely.

They make an excellent team.

Correct errors in subject-verb agreement by crossing through the incorrect verbs and writing in the correct verbs. Follow these instructions for the rest of the exercises in this chapter unless directed to do otherwise. If the subject and verb are in agreement, write a *C* to the right of the sentence.

a. This policy no longer serve the public interest.

b. She don't know how to use the computer.

c. Good communication requires giving attention to detail.

d. You possess the intelligence to succeed in that program.

e. Greenville continue to grow in population.

7-4   When a sentence contains an irregular verb (such as *to be* or *to have*), subject-verb agreement can be difficult to determine. Because irregular verb forms are used frequently, be alert for their proper usage.

7-2

             N
a. Ms. Chandler
    P
b. He
    P
c. You
    N
d. Sean
    P
e. They

FORMS OF *TO BE*

	Singular	Plural
Present Tense:	I *am*	we *are*
	you *are*	you *are*
	he, she, it *is*	they *are*
Past Tense:	I *was*	we *were*
	you *were*	you *were*
	he, she, it *was*	they *were*
Future Tense:	I *will be*	we *will be*
	you *will be*	you *will be*
	he, she, it *will be*	they *will be*

TO HAVE

	Singular	Plural
Present Tense:	I *have*	we *have*
	you *have*	you *have*
	he, she, it *has*	they *have*
Past Tense:	I *had*	we *had*
	you *had*	you *had*
	he, she, it *had*	they *had*
Future Tense:	I *will have*	we *will have*
	you *will have*	you *will have*
	he, she, *it will have*	they *will have*

Proofread for errors in subject-verb agreement by crossing through the incorrect verbs and writing in the correct verb form. If a sentence is correct, write a *C* to the right of it.

a. Mr. Caudell has worked for many years as a police officer.

b. You is responsible for collecting the money.

c. The materials was damaged during the flood.

d. She were supposed to have completed her work by March 1.

e. The representative have decided to resign.

7-5 The subject and the verb must agree in number even though they may be separated by a group of words containing nouns of a different number.

The employees working on that job have to finish it by September 4.

(with S above "employees" and V above "have")

7-3

a. serves
b. doesn't
c. C
d. C
e. continues

S   V
The bus driver, in addition to the students, was injured.

 Proofread for errors in subject-verb agreement. If a sentence is correct, write a *C* to the right of it.

a. The box of Christmas presents was opened by mistake.

b. Money as well as materials are needed for the project.

c. The standards for selecting the candidate is well-defined.

d. The box containing the diskettes was delivered.

e. My friend who works for the social services is being transferred.

7-6 A compound subject (more than one subject) joined by *and* usually requires a plural verb.

S   S   V
Terry Mann and Blair Jordan are seniors.

S   S   V
Chris and I were classmates in school.

Note: When using the pronoun *I* as part of a compound subject, always put the other subject first.

There are only two exceptions to the above rule:

■ When the compound subject is considered to be one unit, use a singular verb.

S   S   V
My teacher and advisor, Dr. Underwood, is a Pirate fan.

■ When the compound subject is preceded by *each, every, many a,* or *many an,* use a singular verb.

S   S   V
Each teacher and student is expected to attend the assembly.

S   S   V
Many an honor and award is presented at graduation.

7-4
a. C
b. **are**
c. **were**
d. **was**
e. **has**

7-5
a. C
b. **is**
c. **are**
d. C
e. C

Proofread for errors in subject-verb agreement. If a sentence is correct, write a *C* to the right of it.

a. Education and experience are prerequisites for most jobs.

b. Our secretary and treasurer, Elena Williams, have resigned.

c. Every state and country has its own flag.

d. Many an author and publisher have responded to the state's requirements.

e. Each cat and dog has to wear an identification collar.

7-7 A compound subject joined by *or* or *nor* may require either a singular verb or a plural verb. The verb should agree with the subject nearest the verb.

    S S V
Either you or I am responsible for paying the bills.

    S   S V
Neither Jon nor they are qualified for that position.

Proofread for errors in subject-verb agreement. If a sentence is correct, write a *C* to the right of it.

a. Neither Mary nor the boys are going to Alaska.

b. Either the butler or the maid are responsible for the dinner.

c. Either Mr. Barclay or his representatives have called the meeting.

d. Neither man, woman, nor child know what the future holds.

e. Either the employer or the employees is going to pay the fee.

7-6

a. C
b. **has**
c. C
d. **has**
e. C

7-8 *There* and *here* are adverbs; therefore, they are never the subject of a sentence. In sentences that begin with *there* or *here*, the subject follows the verb.

V   S
There is an incentive for increased productivity.

V   S   S
Here are an example and an illustration for you to follow.

Proofread for errors in subject-verb agreement. If a sentence is correct, write a *C* to the right of it.

a. There were many injuries as a result of the tornado.

b. Here is the two books that I promised to send.

c. Here is the secretary and treasurer of the company, Mr. Rowe.

d. There are many points to be considered before making the decision.

e. Here is the agenda and feedback reports for the conference.

7-7

a. C
b. **is**
c. C
d. **knows**
e. **are**

7-9   Collective nouns identify groups. When the group acts as one unit, use a singular verb.

S   V
The family is moving to its new home.

S   V
The staff is meeting on Thursday.

■ If the members of the group act individually, use a plural verb.

S   V
The staff are rescheduling their vacations in response to the crisis.

Note: The article preceding the collective noun may indicate whether the group is acting as a unit or individually. *A* usually indicates the need for a plural verb; *the,* a singular verb.

S   V
A number of people are enrolling in the computer classes.

S   V
The number of people enrolling in computer classes is increasing.

7-8

a. C
b. **are**
c. C
d. C
e. **are**

Proofread for errors in subject-verb agreement. If a sentence is correct, write a *C* to the right of it.

   a. The committee has made its decision known to the public.

   b. A number of reasons was given for the decline in the economy.

   c. The audience were very appreciative and applauded vigorously.

   d. Our company has given its employees large bonuses for increased productivity.

   e. The executive board is holding its meeting at the hotel.

7-10 Some pronouns do not refer to definite persons or things. They are called *indefinite pronouns*. The following indefinite pronouns are always singular:

another	everyone	nothing
anyone	everybody	one
anybody	everything	someone
anything	many *a/an*	somebody
each	(see Frame 7-6)	something
either	neither	
every	nobody	
(see Frame 7-6)	no one	

  S   V

Somebody is bringing a stereo to the party.

  S   V

Another one of the companies has put its employees on 12-hour shifts.

■ The following indefinite pronouns are always plural: *both, few, many, others, several.*

  S   V

Both of the computers are used each hour the lab is open.

  S   V

Several were boxed for storage until needed.

7-9

a. C
b. **were**
c. **was**
d. C
e. C

■ The words *all*, *none*, *any*, *more*, *most*, and *some* may be singular or plural depending on how they are used.

    S   V

More than 20 programs were assigned to the class.

    S   V

Some of the paper is being sold at reduced prices.

 Proofread for errors in subject-verb agreement. If a sentence is correct, write a *C* to the right of it.

a. Most of the classes have received new books.

b. Nobody likes to find himself or herself without any money.

c. Each of the performers are very talented.

d. Everyone entering the contest has a chance to win.

e. Neither one of the articles were as well written as it should have been.

Misplaced and Dangling Modifiers

A modifier is a word or group of words that describes. Modifers must be positioned in the sentence so that the intended meaning is clear to the reader. If modifiers are misplaced, who or what performed the action of the sentence is unclear.

7-11 Place modifiers next to, or as close as possible to, the words they modify.

Incorrect: The supervisor issued an electronic typewriter to the secretary with removable storage.

Correct: The supervisor issued an electronic typewriter with removable storage to the secretary.

Note: Check the position of such words as *only*, *at least*, or *merely* to be sure the intended meaning is clear.

Incorrect: Only we paid for the workstation, not the software.

Correct: We paid only for the workstation, not the software.

7-10

a. C
b. C
c. **is**
d. C
e. **was**

- When a modifier does not refer to anything in the sentence, it is termed a *dangling modifier*. Correct dangling modifiers by adding words to make the meaning clear.

Incorrect: While thinking about this catastrophe, the sun sank from view. (The *sun* was not *thinking*.)

Correct: While thinking about this catastrophe, Roger watched the sun sink from view.

Incorrect: Proofreading hurriedly, mistakes were made by the secretary frequently. (*Mistakes* did not *proofread hurriedly* and *frequently* does not modify *secretary*.)

Correct: Proofreading hurriedly, the secretary frequently made mistakes.

Note: An introductory element that describes should be directly followed by the word that it modifies.

 Proofread for misplaced or dangling modifiers. When you find an error, correct the sentence by rearranging the sentence or adding words to make the meaning clear. If a sentence is correct, write a *C* to the right of it.

   a. To determine the value of the car, the Blue Book was consulted by Miss Kornegay.

   b. Grinning from sheer happiness, Kendra ran to meet her fiance.

   c. While working on the manuscript, the word processor continually broke down.

   d. To meet the deadline, all mailings have to be submitted by three o'clock.

   e. Seeing the horse rear up, Jody changed his mind about riding quickly.

Spelling Review

To improve your ability to detect spelling errors, master the words below. Watch for them in the exercises that follow and in succeeding chapters.

bulletin	profited
concession	quantity
emergency	recommendation
necessary	restaurant
pamphlet	unanimous

Proofreading Tips

Study these tips and apply them as you proofread.

1. When determining agreement of subject and verb, be alert for these troublemakers frequently used in business.

   a) Foreign words containing both singular and plural forms:

Singular	Plural
addendum	addenda
analysis	analyses
basis	bases
crisis	crises
criterion	criteria
medium	media
memorandum	memorandums or memoranda
parenthesis	parentheses

   b) Nouns which are spelled the same in both their singular and plural forms:

   means   series

   c) Nouns that are usually considered plural:

credentials	earnings	goods	grounds
premises	proceeds	belongings	

2. As you proofread, adjust your level of effort to the job. A one-time reading of an interoffice memo may be sufficient, but a letter or a report may need to be read more than once.

7-11

a. Miss Kornegay consulted the Blue Book.
b. C
c. While **I was** working on
d. **you must submit** all mailings
e. Jody **quickly** changed

PROOFREADING APPLICATIONS

Proofread the following paragraphs and use the appropriate proofreading symbols to mark errors you find in grammar and spelling. To aid you in proofreading, the number of errors to be found is indicated in parentheses at the end of Exercises P-1, P-2, and P-3. You must find them on your own in Exercise P-4.

P-1 Ellen Webster, president, presided at the September meeting of Phi Beta Lambda. She presented to the membership some recommendations that the executive board had made. Recomendations discussed included holding weekly meetings, having a formal monthly program, and raising money by selling gift items. Neither the president nor the membership were in favor of meeting weekly, but everyone was unaminously in favor of the other two ideas. The president requested that the secretary post a schedule of club events on the bullentin board. (4)

P-1

1. Recommendations
2. membership **was**
3. unanimously
4. bulletin

P-2 Jonathan had a summer job as a marketing trainee for a grocery store. One of his tasks were to prepare a report on what the competition was doing in the city. After obtaining prices for selected items at various stores, the total cost of the items was tallied for each store. This price comparison included only items of comparable size, weight, or quanity, and, wherever possible, the same brand. At the end of the summer, Jonathan acknowledged that he had profitted greatly from this experience. (4)

P-2

1. One of his tasks **was**
2. **he tallied** the total cost
3. quantity
4. profited

P-3 The schedules for outgoing and incoming mail have been changed. To meet the new deadline for outgoing mail, our mailing of sales letters had to be finished by three o'clock. There was only two typists, and they couldn't finish the task alone. Seeing how many letters had to be typed, Mr. Owen called in a typist from another department. Typing rapidly, the letters was finished by the deadline. Teamwork can accomplish what otherwise seems to be impossible. (4)

CHAPTER 7—Proofreading for Grammatical Errors, Part 1

P-4 If your office is typical of most, there's patterns of fluctuation in the flow of work. Even though your secretary plans ahead, a number of unavoidable emergencies is still bound to occur. When you have such an emergency, our temporary employment firm can help you. We will send personnel to your office, or you can send your work to our office. The next time you find it necesary to hire additional help. Please give us a call at 555-1986.

P-3

1. **we had to finish** our mailing
2. There **were** only two
3. **With all three typists** typing rapidly,
4. the letters **were** finished

P-4

1. **there are** patterns
2. emergencies **are** still
3. necessary
4. help, **p**lease give

PROGRESSIVE PROOFREADING

The following section provides an opportunity for you to apply your proofreading skills to a job situation:

You are the office supervisor for the Lawrence Chamber of Commerce. Letters in your office are prepared in the modified block letter style with mixed punctuation. One of your supervisory responsibilities is to check the proofreading skills of your typists and word processing operators. The work of Tyler still needs to be monitored closely. Proofread the following items which were typed by Tyler.

Job 1: Announcement for newspaper prepared from handwritten copy.

Job 2: Letter promoting an amusement park prepared from machine dictation.

Job 3: Letter of invitation prepared from machine dictation.

Job 1   Proofread the typed newspaper announcement by comparing it with the rough draft. Mark your corrections on the typed copy.

The members of the Lawrence Chamber of Commerce invite you to attend their open house in the new building at 1054 Greene Street on Wednesday, October 23, between the hours of 2 p.m. and 5 p.m.

The members of the
Lawrence Chamber of Commerce
invite you
to attend their open house
in the new building at
1045 Green Street
Wednesday, October 23
between 2 and 5 p.m.

Job 2 Typed below is a letter prepared from machine dictation. Using the proofreading symbols you have learned, mark all the errors.

Lawrence Chamber of Commerce
1054 Greene Street
Lawrence, KS 66044-1000
(316) 555-2361

October 18, 19--

Mr. Charles D. Christian
3162 North Tenth Street
Witchita, KS 67203-9149

Dear Mr. Christian:

We are delighted to send you the information you requested
about Queen's Park.

From the map on the enclosed broshure, you can see that
the park is divided into 5 areas. The areas includes
games and rides, exhibits, live entertainment, concession
stands, and a zoo. Something for every member of the
family to enjoy.

On the enclosed list of rates,you will note that persons
under 6 and those over 70 is admitted free. Note, too,
that group rates are available.

The park operates on a daily schedule in the summer but
is open only on weekends during the spring and fall.
Announcements about any special event is placed on the
bullentin board at the entrance to the park.

The enclosed pamplet contains a coupon good for $3 off one
adult admission ticket. Have fun at Queen's Park!

Yours very truly,

Alex F. Stevens, Director

tr

Job 3 Proofread the letter below using the appropriate proofreading symbols to make corrections.

Lawrence Chamber of Commerce
1054 Greene Street
Lawrence, KS 66044-1000
(316) 555-2361

February 10, 19--

Ms. Alita Guitterez, President
National Sales Company, Inc.
3910 Trade Street
Lawrence, KN 66044-5133

Dear Ms. Guitterez:

Welcome to Lawrence! We are delighted that your company chose to locate in our city.

As a member of the business community, you are elegible for membership is the Lawrence Chamber of Commerce. On the first Tuesday of each month,we have a breakfast meeting to which each new businessman and businesswoman are invited. This meeting provides an opportunity for us to get to no each other. Each third Tuesday, we have have a dinner and a business meeting at the Arbor Inn.

We hope your schedule will permit you to attend the next meeting, which will be at Tom's Restaurant on the 6th at 7:30 a.m. The Hospitality Committee are in charge of this function. If you can attend, please call 555-2361.

To welcome you as a new member of the business community, Lawrence Chamber of Commerce's newsletter plans to feature a story about your company in our next issue. Will you submit an article of about 500 words about your company? To meet our deadline, we will need the material by the 25th.

    Again, welcome to our city!

                        Very truly yours,

                        Ms. Cynthia Shepherd,Director
                        Public Relations

tr

Chapter 8

Proofreading for Grammatical Errors, Part 2

Objectives: *After completing this chapter, you should be able to*

1. Identify errors in pronoun-antecedent agreement.
2. Recognize errors in the use of pronoun and case.
3. Identify errors in parallel construction in sentences.
4. Use appropriate proofreading symbols to indicate changes in text.

Grammatical Accuracy

The study of effective communication and proofreading skills continues in Chapter 8. Your grammatical accuracy should improve as pronoun-antecedent agreement, pronoun cases, and parallel structure are reviewed.

Pronoun-Antecedent Agreement

Personal pronouns have various forms to indicate *person* (first person, the person speaking; second person, the person spoken to; and third person, the person spoken about), *number* (singular or plural), and *gender* (masculine, feminine, or neuter). You applied the concept of pronoun number in Chapter 7 when you proofread for errors in subject-verb agreement. In Chapter 8, you will learn to identify errors in agreement of pronouns and the words they refer to and in pronoun selection.

8-1 The word the pronoun refers to is called an *antecedent*. A pronoun must agree with its antecedent in person, number, and gender.

When *Karen* visited, *she* surprised us with a gift.
(third person, singular, feminine)

When *David* visited, *he* surprised us with a gift.
(third person, singular, masculine)

When *Karen and David* visited, *they* surprised us with a gift.
(third person, plural)

8-2 When the antecedent is a collective noun, the proofreader must determine whether the noun represents a group acting as a unit or a group acting as individuals. When the group acts as a unit, use a singular pronoun. When the group acts as individuals, use a plural pronoun.

> The *jury* made *its* decision.
> (group acting as a unit)

> The *staff* submitted *their* vacation schedules.
> (group acting as individuals)

 Proofread the sentences below, inserting the correct pronoun wherever necessary. If a sentence is correct, write a *C* to the right of it.

a. Citizens must pay its taxes by April 15.

b. The girl said she would make the poster.

c. The team won their first game of the season.

d. Paula bought Eddie's car and then sold it to Paula's friend.

e. One of the boys left their coat on the bench.

Pronoun Cases

Pronouns are divided into three different categories according to their use in sentences. These categories are termed *cases* and include the following: subjective, objective, and possessive. A personal pronoun changes its case according to how it is being used. Using the incorrect pronoun case is one of the most common errors made by writers and proofreaders.

8-3 The subjective case pronouns include *I, you, he, she, it, we,* and *they*. Use the subjective case for a pronoun that is the subject of the sentence.

> S   V
> We are making plans for the business seminar.

> S   V
> You are well informed.

> S   S   V
> He and I finished the report.

Note: To determine the correct case when a compound subject is used, consider each subject alone with the verb. You would say "I finished the report," not "Me finished the report."

8-1—8-2
their
a. ~~its~~

b. C
     its
c. ~~their~~
       her
d. ~~Paula's~~
     his
e. ~~their~~

■ Use the subjective case when the pronoun refers to the subject and follows a form of the verb *to be (be, am, is, are, was, were)* or a verb phrase ending in *be, being,* or *been.*

> It is *I.*

> It was *she* who found the solution to the problem.

> It could have been *they* who won.

Note: This sentence, while grammatically correct, is awkward. Normally it is best to reword to avoid such constructions: They could have won.

Proofread the sentences below inserting the correct pronoun wherever necessary. If a sentence is correct, write a *C* to the right of it.

a. It was her who wrote the letter.

b. Us secretaries are loyal to our employers.

c. It is he who is responsible for the program.

d. It must have been her who left the message.

e. If you were he, you would do the job now.

8-4   The objective case pronouns include *me, us, you, him, her, it,* and *them.* Use the objective case when the pronoun is the object of the verb. A pronoun is an object if it (1) follows the verb and answers the question "what" or "whom" about the verb or if it (2) follows the verb and answers the question "to whom," "for whom," or "for what" something is done.

> John asked *us* for a contribution.
> (Asked whom?)

> Please put *them* in the file.
> (Put what?)

> Sarah gave *him* and *me* a pen.
> (Gave to whom?)

> Michael bought *them* tickets.
> (Bought for whom?)

■ Use the objective case when the pronoun is the object of the preposition. A pronoun is the object of the preposition if the pronoun follows a preposition (like *among, at, between, by, for, from, on, to,* and *with*).

> This telegram came for *us* today.

> Just between *you* and *me,* I think it is a great idea.

8-3

a. **she**
b. **We**
c. C
d. **she**
e. C

■ Use the objective case when the pronoun is the subject or object of an infinitive. An infinitive is a phrase containing the word *to* plus the present form of a verb. When a pronoun immediately precedes or follows an infinitive phrase, the objective form of the pronoun should be used.

> Stephanie expected *them* to help.
> (*Them* is the subject of the infinitive.)

> Stephanie expected to help *them*.
> (To help whom? *Them* is the object of the infinitive.)

 Proofread the sentences below, inserting the correct pronoun where necessary. If a sentence is correct, write a *C* to the right of it.

   a. He saw her at the symphony concert.

   b. James introduced me to Ruth and she.

   c. Mr. Rosenbloom asked Miss Connair and her to attend the meeting.

   d. He asked me to help with the registration.

   e. Let's send a copy of the report to Kate and he.

8-4
a. C
b. **her**
c. C
d. C
e. **him**

8-5   While it may appear difficult to master, usage of the pronouns *who* and *whom*, *whoever* and *whomever* is really quite simple. Whenever *who* or *whom* appears in a dependent clause, determine the pronoun's use within the clause. Do not consider the rest of the sentence. (A dependent clause contains a subject and a verb but does not express a complete thought.)

■ *Who* and *whoever* are the subjective forms. Use *who* whenever *he, she, they, I,* or *we* could be used as the subject of the *who* clause.

> An executive wants a secretary **who** *is dependable.*
> (*He* is dependable.)

> *Who* shall I say is calling?
> (I shall say *she* is calling.)

> **Whoever** *ate the fruit* should replace it.
> (*They* should replace it.)

Note: If the sentence is a question, mentally change the question to a statement. Then substitute *he/she/they* or *him/her/them* for *who* or *whom*.

■ *Whom* and *whomever* are the objective forms. Use *whom* whenever *him, her, them, me,* or *us* could be used as the object of the verb or the object of a preposition in the *whom* clause.

The person **whom** *you recommended* for the position starts work tomorrow.
(You recommended *her*.)

Whom did you wish to speak *with*?
(You wished to speak with *him*.)

We will promote **whomever** *you suggest*.
(You suggest *him*.)

Choose the correct pronoun in each sentence; then circle it.

a. For (who, whom) did you vote for mayor?

b. Kecia is a person (who, whom) I think will be dependable.

c. Dale is one (who, whom) is going to run for public office.

d. The artist to (who, whom) the award was given is a local person.

e. We have respect for (whoever, whomever) is in charge.

8-6 Use the possessive case to show ownership. Possessive case pronouns usually have two forms.

■ Use *my, your, his, her, its, our,* or *their* when the possessive pronoun precedes the noun it modifies.

That is *my* piano.

It was *their* fault.

■ Use *mine, yours, his, hers, its, ours,* or *theirs* when the possessive pronoun is separated from the noun to which it refers.

That piano is *mine*.

The fault was not *theirs*.

Each idea has *its* own merit.

Note: Do not confuse possessive pronouns such as *its, your,* and *their* with soundalike contractions such as *it's, you're,* and *they're*.

8-5
a. whom
b. who
c. who
d. whom
e. whoever

■ Use the possessive case of a pronoun immediately before a gerund (a verb form ending in *-ing* that is used as a noun).

> *His* leaving the company was a surprise.

> The teacher approved of *our* going on the field trip.

 Proofread the following sentences for errors in pronoun selection. If a sentence is correct, write a *C* to the right of it.

a. That is you gift, not mine.

b. Her leaving the company came at a difficult time.

c. The president, as well as the board members, has stated his opposition to this change.

d. Because the policy was a reasonable one, the staff favored it's adoption.

e. She will appreciate your filling the order at once.

Parallel Construction

Within a sentence, related ideas should be expressed in similar grammatical form. The expression of related ideas in a similar fashion is known as *parallel construction*. Such construction helps to emphasize the connection between thoughts in a sentence and contributes to ease in reading. For this reason, a good proofreader must learn to spot and correct sentences that are not parallel in structure.

8-7 Within each sentence, balance an adjective with an adjective, a phrase with a phrase, and a clause with a clause.

Incorrect: A receptionist's duties include *answering the* telephone and *the sorting of the* mail.

Correct: A receptionist's duties include *answering the* telephone and *sorting the* mail.

Incorrect: What *we think* and the *things we say* are often not the same.

Correct: What *we think* and what *we say* are often not the same.

8-8 Conjunctions used in pairs (both . . . and, either . . . or, neither . . . nor, not only . . . but also, whether . . . or) should be followed by words in the same grammatical form.

8-6

a. your
b. C
c. C
d. **its**
e. C

Incorrect: The college offers both *a degree in word processing* and *engineering*.

Correct: The college offers a degree in both *word processing* and *engineering*.

Incorrect: Freshmen not only *are* insecure but also *naive*.

Correct: Freshmen are not only *insecure* but also *naive*.

 Proofread the sentences below, correcting the structure where it is not parallel. If a sentence is correct, write a *C* to the right of it.

a. Carole's goals are to increase her dictation speed and improving accuracy of her transcripts.

b. Neither the car nor the van would start this cold morning.

c. The view of the mountains is breathtaking and an inspiration.

d. The film not only frightened the children but also their parents.

e. Audrey's interests include reading and to do painting.

Spelling Review

To improve your ability to detect spelling errors, master the words below. Watch for them in the exercises that follow and in succeeding chapters.

criticism	possession
enthusiasm	recognize
incidentally	regard
miscellaneous	relevant
permanent	responsible

Proofreading Tips

Study these tips and apply them as you proofread:

1. If you spot a grammatical error, write a question mark in the margin next to the sentence and query the originator.

2. Reading aloud to yourself is a good way to detect grammatical errors.

8-7—8-8

a. **to improve** the accuracy

b. C

c. **inspiring**

d. **frightened not only**

e. and painting

PROOFREADING APPLICATIONS

Proofread the following paragraphs and use the appropriate proofreading symbols to mark errors you find in spelling and grammar. To aid you in proofreading, the number of errors to be found is indicated in parentheses at the end of Exercises P-1, P-2, and P-3. You must find them on your own in Exercise P-4.

P-1   I am happy to recommend Ms. Lao, about who you inquired in your letter of October 30. Ms. Lao was employed as a supervisor in our company for three years. It was her who developed the training plan that we are using. Ms. Lao is a capable person with a number of outstanding qualities. Among them are excellent organizational skills, good human relations skills, a strong sense of enthuziasm, and being creative. (4)

P-2   Copies of the book you requested are being sent to Mr. Durham and he today. We hope this book will be helpful to them in their work. It not only is relevent but also beautifully illustrated. The publishing company hired a well-known artist to produce its artwork, and she did an excellent job. We're sure that the book will become a valued possession. (3)

P-3   Sam Quincy and me have opened an advertising agency in the Brendle Building. Me and he think that it will provide a much-needed service in our town. We also believe it's location will be an asset since it's near the major business district. Also, with the establishment of several new businesses in our area, we expect the agency to gain many new clients. (3)

P-1

1. about **whom**
2. It was **she**
3. enthusiasm
4. and **creativity**

P-2

1. Mr. Durham and **him**
2. It **is** not only
3. rele**v**ant

P-4   I appreciate you sending me the article about why employers prefer high school graduates who have had vocational courses. It confirms some of my own ideas. All high school graduates cannot, should not, and will not go to college; but all of them will need marketable skills. Employers recognise that prospective employees who have had vocational courses will not only have marketable skills but also better attitudes, good human relations skills, and will have an appreciation for work.

P-3

1. and **I** have
2. **He** and **I** think
3. believe **its**

P-4

1. **your** sending
2. recognize
3. will **have** not only
4. **and** an appreciation

PROGRESSIVE PROOFREADING

The following section provides an opportunity for you to apply your proofreading skills to a job situation:

You have applied for a position as a secretary in the School of Technology at City College. Dr. Brian Layman, your prospective employer, is seeking a person who has exceptionally good language arts skills. To determine whether you can do the job, you are given some drafts of correspondence to proofread. Dr. Layman uses the block letter style with mixed punctuation.

Job 1: Letter to Phi Beta Lambda sponsor.

Job 2: Memorandum about establishment of a task force.

Job 3: Memorandum about parking regulations.

Job 1   Proofread the letter below.

**School of Technology
City College**

989 Johnstown Road
Chesapeake, VA 23310-4961

August 29, 19--

Mr. Herbert Smiley
358 Bartell Drive
Chesepeake, VA 23320-8765

Dear Herb:

For several reasons, Tracy and I think you, as sponsor, should
attend the regional Phi Beta Lambda Conference in lieu of either
her or me. First, since you are more familar with the organization,
you would profit more form the program and could share the information with the members of the club who are preparing for the state
contests.

Second, since one part of the program will be devoted to the duties
of the sponsor, you would logically benefit more from this information
than any of we others. These reasons suggest to Tracy and I that
you should represent our group.

    Should you decide to attend, please contact me at 555-1932.
If you do attend, you will be reimbursed for your expenses. Just
be sure to report your expenses to Dr. Clark or his secretary upon
your return.

Incidently, if anyone asks, you can say that it was me who suggested you going.

                        Very sincerely yours,

                        Mary M. McGuestin

RV

Job 2 Proofread the memorandum to all staff members.

School of Technology
City College

Internal Memorandum

TO: All Staff

FROM: Brian Layman, Dean

DATE: August 29, 19--

SUBJECT: Establishment of Task Force

At the suggestion of numerous staff members, the university is pursuing the idea of purchasing a computer system for general use. Members of the staff with who I have talked have shown many applications for computer useage in your daily work.

A task force of interested staff members are being formed to conduct a more through study of the needs of the staff. Based on its findings, the task force will then make recommendations for the purchase of a computer system and software. I need to know who among the staff are interested in serving on the task force.

Responsibilities of the task force includes the following: (1) assessing the staff's needs, (2) gathering information about computer systems, (3) evaluating the software available, and (4) to make recommendations to the purchasing agent and I.

If your interested in actively researching this topic and meeting this challenge, please send me a memo indicating your interest.

rv

Job 3 As you proofread, note any errors in typing, spelling, and grammar. Show your knowledge about these areas by finding all of the errors.

 School of Technology City College

Internal Memorandum

TO: Department Charipersons

FROM: Brian Layman, Dean

DATE: August 29, 19--

SUBJECT: Parking Regulations

In an effort to improve staff parking conditions, the Campus Traffic Committee have developed the following parking regulations. Will you please see that all members of your department receives this information reguarding the new regulations.

1. All current campus parking permits expire on September 14. Beginning September 15, new permits are required for we staff members.

2. Parking is prohibited in areas other then those designated for staff members.

3. Parking is prohibited in metered areas.

4. Parking regulations must be observed in locations where specific hours are listed.

5. Permanant premits must be displayed in the rear window of all vechicles.

6. Campus security officers will issue tickets to those who violate the parking regulations.

Because Chief Security Officer Calder has been aware of the miscelaneous problems in parking, he was very receptive to the recommendations made by the staff members who comprised the committee. In fact, it was him who suggested a number of the new regulations.

Department Chairpersons
Page 2
August 29, 19--

Officer Calder and the members of the Traffic Committee is sure
that the members of your department, as responsable college em-
employees, will cooperate by adhering to these regulations. If
you become aware of any criticism of the new regulations, please
let me know--the college administration welcomes and recognizes
employee comments and suggestions.

rv

Chapter 9

Proofreading for Confusing Words

Objectives: *After completing this chapter, you should be able to*

1. Recognize the correct usage of words that sound alike but have different meanings.
2. Recognize the correct spelling of words that sound alike but have different spellings.
3. Use appropriate proofreading symbols to indicate changes in text.

One of the major difficulties of the English language is that so many words sound similar but are spelled differently and have different meanings. To be a good proofreader, you must be able to distinguish between those words of similar sound and spelling so that you will be able to detect and correct errors in their usage. Study each group of words and their definitions. Then read each of the sentences, and write the correct word in the space provided.

9-1   accept—*v*. to receive; to take
except—*prep*. with the exclusion of

a. You should _____ the responsibility for completing the payroll.

b. All of the officers _____ the secretary attended the meeting.

c. We will fight the courts about the ruling rather than _____ it.

d. No one _____ the treasurer can unlock the bank vault.

9-2 addition—*n.* increase; enlargement or gain
edition—*n.* form in which a text is published

a. In six months the new _____ to the office building will be completed.

b. She autographed a copy of the latest _____ of her book.

c. Do you think the _____ to the laboratory will be approved?

d. Since the _____ of Mario to the staff, we have caught up with our work.

9-3 advice—*n.* recommendation; suggestion
advise—*v.* to counsel; to inform

a. When I _____ you on financial matters, I think you should take the _____.

b. The counselor gives excellent _____ to clients.

c. You should _____ us about the forwarding of your mail.

d. His _____ about the computer software was most welcome.

9-4 affect—*v.* to influence
effect—*n.* an outcome or a result; *v.* to cause to happen

a. What _____ will the change in the law have on us?

b. Your performance will _____ your rating.

c. The plans to _____ a change in policy have been approved.

d. How will her resignation _____ our previous plans?

9-1

a. accept
b. except
c. accept
d. except

9-2

a. addition
b. edition
c. addition
d. addition

9-3

a. advise and advice
b. advice
c. advise
d. advice

9-5   a lot—*n.* a number of; many
allot—*v.* to assign; to distribute

> a. The hotel will _____ ten meeting rooms for our conference.
>
> b. Did you find _____ of errors in the transcription paper?
>
> c. We will _____ 5 percent of the total amount for printing expenses.
>
> d. There are _____ of people who are uncomfortable working with computers.

9-6   all ready—*adj. phrase* completely prepared
already—*adv.* by or before this time

> a. Since the contract had _____ been signed, the engineer could begin to work.
>
> b. Paul had the letters _____ to be mailed before noon.
>
> c. The student had _____ been notified about the scholarship nomination.
>
> d. An increase in holiday sales had _____ been predicted.

9-7   cite—*v.* to quote or mention
sight—*n. a* view; vision; *v.* to see
site—*n.* a location

> a. Can you _____ the source of that quotation?
>
> b. As soon as the company finds the proper _____, it will begin construction of its building.
>
> c. The Grand Canyon is an inspiring _____.
>
> d. The coliseum is located on a _____ about three blocks away.

9-4

a. effect
b. affect
c. effect
d. affect

9-5

a. allot
b. a lot
c. allot
d. a lot

9-6

a. already
b. all ready
c. already
d. already

9-8 complement—*n.* something that fills up, completes, or makes perfect; *v.* to complete or make perfect

complement—*n.* recognition; *v.* praise; to praise

a. Did you _____ the actor on his performance?

b. The drapes and the carpet _____ the color of the walls.

c. I consider that remark to be a _____.

d. When the ship left the shore, it had a full _____ of personnel.

9-9 council—*n.* an assembly; a governing body

counsel—*v.* to give advice; advise; *n.* a lawyer; advice

a. Who was appointed _____ for the defense?

b. The _____ that his parents gave him was to work hard.

c. Karly served for two years as president of the student _____.

d. Did you know there are more women than men on the city _____?

9-10 envelop—*v.* to surround; to enclose

envelope—*n.* a flat (usually paper) container for a letter

a. If the fog continues, it will quickly _____ the entire area.

b. Use the enclosed _____ for mailing your contribution.

c. While disciplining your children, _____ them with love.

d. Why not use a small _____ for returning the copy of the receipt?

9-7

a. cite
b. site
c. sight
d. site

9-8

a. compliment
b. complement
c. compliment
d. complement

9-9

a. counsel
b. counsel
c. council
d. council

9-11 every day—*adv. phrase* each day
everyday—*adj.* ordinary; customary

a. The girls have been jogging _____ this week.

b. Proofreading is an _____ task for the word processing secretary.

c. Why not use the _____ dishes for the picnic?

d. When you retire from your job, _____ will be a holiday!

9-12 its—*adj.* possessive form of *it*
it's—contraction of *it is* and *it has*

a. When _____ 7 p.m. in Knoxville, the sun is still shining in Phoenix.

b. The company has been sued by one of _____ creditors for nonpayment.

c. _____ been almost four years since you entered college.

d. Was the machine put back in _____ case?

9-13 loose—*adj.* not fastened or tight; having freedom of movement
lose—*v.* to fail to win, gain, or keep; to mislay

a. Too many traffic violations caused Kevin to _____ his license.

b. When the belt is too _____, it will not pull the motor.

c. The loss of the key will cause us to _____ access to the safe-deposit box.

d. We lost several pages of the book when its binding came _____.

9-10

a. envelop
b. envelope
c. envelop
d. envelope

9-11

a. every day
b. everyday
c. everyday
d. every day

9-12

a. it's
b. its
c. It's
d. its

9-14   moral—*adj.* ethical; pertaining to right and wrong
         morale—*n.* a mental and emotional condition; mood

a. Keeping up the _____ of its employees is important to a company.

b. Today's society has to face several _____ issues.

c. After its third loss, the tennis team's _____ was pretty low.

d. One admirable trait is that of high _____ standards.

9-15   passed—*v.* past tense of *pass,* meaning to go by or to
         circumvent
       past—*n.* the time before the present; *adv.* go beyond

a. President Reagan went _____ the school on his way to Camp David.

b. We were traveling so fast that we _____ the entrance to the park.

c. All of the students in the ten o'clock class _____ the first test.

d. We must know the _____ so we can appreciate the present.

9-16   personal—*adj.* private; relating to an individual
         personnel—*n.* a body of employees

a. I wish to obtain a _____ loan from the bank.

b. Katie had an interview with the head of the _____ department.

c. All of the company _____ received end-of-the-year bonuses.

d. Employers are not permitted to ask their employees for certain _____ information.

9-13

a. lose
b. loose
c. lose
d. loose

9-14

a. morale
b. moral
c. morale
d. moral

9-15

a. past
b. passed
c. passed
d. past

CHAPTER 9—Proofreading for Confusing Words

9-17   precede—*v.* to go or come before or in front of
preceding—*adj.* previous
proceed—*v.* to move forward; advance

a. Mikki Parker _____ Ms. Brumfield as principal.

b. Can you apply the procedures you learned in the _____ lesson?

c. The council will _____ to the next item on the agenda.

d. The second edition has enjoyed over $375,000 in sales this year; that is more than the sales for the two _____ years.

9-16

a. personal
b. personnel
c. personnel
d. personal

9-18   principal—*n.* a leader; a sum of money; *adj.* highest in importance
principle—*n.* a general truth; an accepted truth

a. Did you hear the _____ singing in her office?

b. The _____ of supply and demand is only one aspect of economic theory.

c. "It is not the money; it's the _____ of the matter" is a well-known saying.

d. Discussing the office of the future was the _____ topic of the meeting.

9-17

a. preceded
b. preceding
c. proceed
d. preceding

9-19   sales—*n.* distribution by selling; *adj.* relating to or used in selling
sells—*v.* achieves a sale, exacts a price for

a. The _____ tax adds 5 percent to the cost of the goods.

b. Bradley will win a cruise if he _____ nine cars this month.

c. The store's charge _____ have doubled in the past five years.

d. To earn extra income, Margo _____ stationery products.

9-18

a. principal
b. principle
c. principle
d. principal

9-20

stationary—*adj.* immobile; fixed in one position
stationery—*n.* materials (paper, pens, ink) for writing

a. That card shop also sells _____.

b. Every physical fitness enthusiast should have a _____ bicycle.

c. In the business world the use of colored _____ appears to be a trend.

d. Nailing the desk to the floor will certainly keep it _____.

9-21

their—*adj.* the possessive form of *they*
there—*adv.* at that place; *pron.* used as an introductory word in a sentence
they're—contraction of *they are*

a. The twins were standing _____ by the door when I left.

b. Next year _____ going to remodel the entire building.

c. Seven employees celebrated _____ retirement from the company.

d. During spring vacation _____ going to see _____ relatives.

9-22

to—*prep.* in the direction of; indicates an infinitive
too—*adv.* also; more than enough
two—*adj.* more than one but less than three

a. Lisa and I are going, _____, if there's room.

b. Did you know that only _____ candidates showed up for the forum?

c. "_____ be rather than _____ seem" is the motto of what state?

d. He, _____, can go to the _____ day conference if he can get someone _____ drive him there.

9-19

a. sales
b. sells
c. sales
d. sells

9-20

a. stationery
b. stationary
c. stationery
d. stationary

9-21

a. there
b. they're
c. their
d. they're and their

CHAPTER 9—Proofreading for Confusing Words

Spelling Review

To improve your ability to detect spelling errors, master the words below. Watch for them in the exercises that follow and in succeeding chapters.

experience	psychology
grammar	receiving
occasionally	reference
omitted	valuable
prerequisite	writing

Proofreading Tips

Study these tips and apply them as you proofread:

1. When in doubt about the meaning or spelling of a word, consult the dictionary. The correct word usage shows that you have proofread all communications carefully so that the reader can understand the intended message.

2. Be aware of the standard pronunciation of words because mispronunciation frequently leads to misspelling and misuse of words.

9-22

a. too
b. two
c. To and to
d. too, two, and to

PROOFREADING APPLICATIONS

Proofread the following paragraphs and use the appropriate proofreading symbols to mark errors you find in word usage or spelling. To aid you in proofreading, the number of errors to be found is indicated in parentheses at the end of Exercises P-1, P-2, and P-3. You must find them on your own in Exercise P-4.

P-1 There is much dissatisfaction about the proposed site for the new building. The council members think that there is not enough room for parking in that area because there are two many buildings there already. What effect would the proposed site have on business? What would you advice the committee to do? Since the members respect your knowlidge of these matters, I believe they would except your ideas. (4)

P-2 Upon recieving his annual seed catalog, Grandfather said it was a reminder that it's time for him to decide what flowers to order for his garden. He especially likes crocuses and jonquils. They are the first flowers to bloom in the new year, and they brighten the landscape every day for about a two-week period. These flowers are colorful editions to Grandfather's yard, and there beauty lifts his moral. Grandfather was prepared to write his order but discovered that the order blank had been omitted or had come lose from the catalog. Therefore, he used the company's toll-free telephone number to place his order. (5)

P-3 At my first job interview, I noticed that there were alot of other applicants there to. Although I was nervous, Mrs. Gloria Nespal, the interviewer, soon made me feel at ease. She complimented me on my personal appearance and on the quality of stationery I had used for my application papers. As she looked at them, she noticed the principle courses I had taken (psycology was one) and commented about there relationship to the job I was seeking. After some questioning, Mrs. Nespal requested that I supply an additional referance, and the interview was over. I felt as if I had past it! Now I'm waiting for that envelope containing a letter saying, "The job is yours!" (7)

P-1

1. **too** many
2. **advise** the committee
3. **knowledge**
4. **acc**ept

P-2

1. rec**ei**ving
2. colorful **additions**
3. **their** beauty
4. mora**le**
5. lo**o**se

P-4 If you have excelled in the position of legal secretary, your employer will likely council you to consider the challenge of becoming a paralegal assistant. The expereince you have gained as a legal secretary will serve as a foundation for the advanced training. You have, no doubt, developed the necessary grammer and writeing skills; and you probably have done legal research. Occasionally you may have drafted wills. You have, in fact, already acquired some of the skills of the paralegal assistant. Why not obtain the formal training that will enable you to increase your responsibilities and your pay?

P-3

1. were **a lot** of other
2. there to**o**.
3. princi**pal** courses
4. psycho**l**ogy
5. th**ei**r relationship
6. refere**n**ce
7. pa**ssed** it

P-4

1. coun**sel** you
2. exper**ie**nce you
3. gram**mar** and
4. writ**ing** skills

PROGRESSIVE PROOFREADING

The following section provides an opportunity for you to apply your proofreading skills to a job situation:

One of your duties as a clerical supervisor in the Hartsell Real Estate office is to proofread the work of the typists. You proofread not only for the usual typographical and spelling errors but also for errors in grammar and word usage. As you proofread the following papers, use the proper proofreading marks and mark all the errors. Hartsell uses modified block letter style and mixed punctuation.

Job 1: Memorandum of congratulations.

Job 2: Letter to a client.

Job 3: Letter of recommendation.

Job 1 Mark all errors on the following memorandum using the appropriate proofreading symbols.

Hartsell Real Estate

Internal Memorandum

TO: Hannah Silverthorne

FROM: Walter T. Hartsell

DATE: July 14, 19--

SUBJECT: Sales Quota Exceeded

Congradulations on your success not only in reaching but also
in exceeding your sales quota for the passed six months. In view
of the sluggish market during this period, I realize it's taken
alot of personal effort to reach this goal.

Your performance demonstrates that you believe in the principle
that what is good for business is good for you. Cold canvassing is never easy, but your attitude shows that your objective
is to sell property, not to avoid failure--to gain valueable experience, not to maintain the status quo. The net affect of your
efforts are that we will not loose our No. 1 ranking in the city.

Thank you, Hannah, for your contributions; your enthusasm is contagious. I'm proud to have you on our sales force.

yri

Job 2 Proofread the letter below to Mr. Whitehurst, client.

Hartsell Real Estate

1760 Asbury Street
Indianapolis, IN 46203-3952

                                        July 19, 19--

        Mr. Bryant Whitehurst
        Plant Manager
        Toggs Manufacturing Co.
        P. O. Box 7022
        Indianapolis, IN 46208-9865

        Dear Mr. Whitehurst:

        The one hundred-acre sight on Five-Mile Rd. you wanted
        for your new plant is available. Even though the owners
        have all ready had a lot of inquiries about the property,
        I believe they're prepared to accept your proposed offer.

        If you are serious about obtaining this property, I sug-
        gest that you submit an offer immediately. Real estate
        prices are not likely to decrease further this year. In
        fact, it is likely to increase.

        Because the owners insist on a cash transaction, you may
        want to get your counsel's advise about the best way to
        finance the principal loan. Please call me to discuss
        your plans about this matter.

                                        Sincerely yours,

                                        Walter T. Hartsell
                                        General Manager

        yri

Job 3   Proofread the following letter of recommendation.

Hartsell Real Estate
1760 Asbury Street
Indianapolis, IN 46203-3952

July 14, 19--

Miss Kimary Etheridge
Personnel Director
Merritt Electronic Co.
7643 Evans Avenue
Gainesville, Florida 32612-9876

Dear Ms. Kimary:

I was surprised to learn that Ms. Melanie Cooke has used
my name as a referance on her application for a job with
your company.

Ms. Cooke worked with me for about 3 months. During
that time her work was never up to the standards demanded
by business. My major critacism of her as an employee
centered on her carelessness and inefficiency in her work.

Ms. Cooke frequently arrived late or left early. She was
careless in her personel appearance, and her overall attitude was not good. After speaking to her on several occassions about her lack of efficiency and then noting no
improvement, I was forced to dismiss her.

Had Ms. Cooke requested permission to use my name as a
referance, I would have declined; but since she did not,
I have no alternative but to give her an unsatisfactory
recommendation.

                         Sincerely yours,

                         Walter T. Hartsell
                         General Manager

yri

Proofreading for Punctuation Errors, Part 1

Objectives: *After completing this chapter, you should be able to*

1. Identify errors in end-of-sentence punctuation.
2. Identify errors in the use of the comma in compound sentences, in a series, with consecutive adjectives, with adjacent numbers, and in dates and addresses.
3. Use appropriate proofreading symbols to indicate changes in text.

Importance of Correct Punctuation

Punctuation makes the meaning of messages clear and precise. When punctuation is omitted or used incorrectly, messages may become confusing, distorted, or inaccurate. Consider the change in meaning in the following sentences:

"The child," claimed the newscaster, "was abducted by an angry mob."

The child claimed the newscaster was abducted by an angry mob.

It is essential that the proofreader know how to use the different marks of punctuation.

In this chapter you will review the correct use of terminal punctuation (punctuation used at the end of a sentence) and the most common internal punctuation mark, the comma. Additional uses of the comma and other internal punctuation are reviewed in Chapters 11 and 12.

Terminal Punctuation

Terminal punctuation is used to indicate a distinct pause in the voice and thus helps to clarify the meaning of sentences. Terminal punctuation marks consist of the period, the question mark, and the exclamation point. Internal punctuation marks, which will be discussed later in the chapter, signify shorter pauses and help to further clarify the meaning.

Use the following proofreading symbols to indicate changes in punctuation.

⊙   Insert a period.

`May has been beautiful⊙`

?/   Insert a question mark.

`Are you going to the wedding?/`

!/   Insert an exclamation point.

`She will be raising a gorilla!/`

10-1 Use a period at the end of a statement or a command, a polite request, or an indirect question.

> It is a beautiful day.
> (statement of fact)
>
> Be sure to make the reservation this morning.
> (command)
>
> I asked if she had eaten.
> (indirect question)

■ Remember to use a period rather than a question mark if the reader is requested to act rather than to answer.

> Will you please make a copy of this letter.
> (polite request, action required)
>
> Did you go to the dance?
> (direct question, answer required)

10-2 Use a question mark after a direct question. The first word of a direct question is capitalized.

> Did you proofread carefully?
>
> The question is, Which is the best software?

■ Use a question mark after each item in a series of short questions related to one idea. Begin each question in a series with lower-case letters if it is not a complete sentence. One space follows all but the final question mark.

Is your objective to avoid failure? to protect your ego? to sell property?

Who proofread this? Was it Mary? Was it Aaron?

10-3

Use an exclamation point to express intense feeling or to give emphasis after an interjection. One space follows an exclamation point if it appears within a sentence.

John won the lottery!

Congratulations! You have completed your coursework.

One of the parachutes hasn't opened!

 Proofread the following groups of words for errors in terminal punctuation. If a sentence is correct, write a *C* to the right of it.

a. Will you kindly move to the end of the line?

b. You may well ask what the procedure for payment is when registering late.

c. I can't believe English 201 is already closed!

d. Which class will you substitute? business communication? marketing?

e. The assistant exclaimed, "Finally. The last schedule has been processed!"

Internal Punctuation—The Comma

Internal punctuation is used when a brief pause, rather than a distinct pause, is needed. Internal punctuation marks consist of the comma (discussed below), the colon, the semicolon, the dash, parentheses, quotation marks, the underscore, and the apostrophe (all discussed in Chapter 12), each of which has a specific function. The proofreader should know the function of each mark of punctuation and keep in mind that it is used to make the meaning clearer.

Use the following proofreading symbols to mark corrections in the use of the comma.

⋏   Insert a comma.

We are attending the conference in Kansas City⋏and then we will go on to Los Angeles.

⊘   Delete a comma.

The children are opening their gifts⊘ and sharing their toys.

10-1—10-3

a. line.

b. C

c. C

d. C

e. Finally.
processed.

10-4

Use a comma to separate the main clauses of a compound sentence connected by the conjunctions *and, or, but,* or *nor.* (A compound sentence consists of two main clauses, each containing both a subject and a verb.) The comma comes before the conjunction.

S V   S   V
I am not a member of that group, nor do I intend to become a member.

        S   V   S V
The delegation met for two hours, but it took no action on the issue of sanctions.

      S   V   S   V
Betty Robbins will attend the meeting, or she will send a substitute.

■ If both clauses are short, do not use a comma.

        S   V   S   V
        Cindy typed the report and Larry mailed it.
            (short, compound sentence)

Note: Do not mistake a compound sentence for a simple sentence with two or more verbs. Such a sentence requires no comma before the conjunction.

      S   V   V
The telephone transmits important business messages and allows friends to keep in touch.
    (simple sentence containing one subject and two verbs)

Proofread the following sentences for errors in the use of the comma. If a sentence is correct, write a *C* to the right of it.

a. Many people do not understand the benefits that a humidifier offers, nor are they willing to take the time to learn.

b. A humidifier will permit the thermostat to be set lower, but it will not work effectively if the temperature is too low.

c. A humidifier can relieve severe congestion, and soothe the dry throats that prompt coughing.

d. Low humidity allows static electricity to build up, and it accounts for minor electrical shocks received when touching a metal object.

e. An acceptable humidity range is between 40 and 60 percent but higher ranges may cause paper to absorb moisture.

10-5 Use the comma to separate three or more elements in a series. Use a comma before the conjunction preceding the last item in the series.

We sell groceries, clothes, hardware, and garden supplies in our store. (word series)

Tom, Dave, and Paul attended the game. (proper noun series)

They picked up the tickets, attended the movie, and returned home that night. (phrase series)

Jim cooked, Bob ate, and Susie cleaned up. (clause series)

Proofread the following sentences for errors in the use of the comma. If a sentence is correct, write a *C* to the right of it.

a. A recruiting drive is on for artists, students, homemakers and unemployed executives willing to work as temporary employees.

b. This trend is increasing because hiring costs are less, fringe benefits do not have to be provided and workloads can be handled more easily in peak periods.

c. Temporaries are being hired to do accounting, programming, engineering, legal work and other jobs that ordinarily command higher pay.

d. More people are turning to temporary work because of the freedom, and flexibility it provides.

e. Medical, technical, and professional temporaries account for 31 percent of the temporary workforce.

10-4

a. C
b. C
c. congestion and
d. C
e. percent, but

10-6 Use a comma to separate two consecutive adjectives that modify the same noun. A comma is needed between the two adjectives if they can be joined by *and*.

This has been a long, hard trip. (long and hard)

She bought a good used car.
(*Good* modifies the idea expressed by the combination *used car*. It is not a good *and* used car.)

 Proofread the following sentences for errors in the use of commas. If a sentence is correct, write a *C* to the right of it.

a. Real estate offers a rich rewarding career.

b. We often associate a residential real estate agent with signs posted on local front lawns.

c. Most real estate agents are concentrated in large, urban areas or in small but rapidly growing communities.

d. Many jobs exist in real estate if you consider the total career area.

e. An up-to-date, annotated reference on jobs in real estate can be found in your local library.

10-7 Use a comma to separate unrelated adjacent numbers.

On page 15, 35 different kinds of birds are named.

■ Use a comma to separate numbers with four or more digits, unless the number identifies (such as an invoice number) rather than enumerates.

A balance of $2,500 is due on Invoice 67412.

10-8 Use a comma to separate parts of addresses and dates.

The meeting was held Sunday, November 15, 1987, at 1 p.m.
We visited Washington, D.C., this summer.

10-5

a. homemakers, and
b. provided, and
c. legal work, and
d. freedom and
e. C

10-6

a. rich, rewarding
b. C
c. large urban areas
d. C
e. C

Spring practice will be held in Toronto, Canada, this year.

Please send the shipment to Mark Dues, 528 Easy Street, Sunnyvale, CA 94088-9236.

Note: The comma may be omitted when only the month and year are given.

The next seminar will be held in June 1988 in Seattle.

 Proofread the following paragraph for errors in the use of the comma.

> Shoe factories from Springfield, Missouri, to Bangor, Maine have been closed because of competition from imports. One shoe company that previously hired about 850 workers and made 10000 shoes a day now has about 325 employees and makes 2,200 shoes daily. According to the figures given on page 12 17 factories have been forced to close within the past six months.

Spelling Review

To improve your ability to detect spelling errors, master the words below. Watch for them in the exercises that follow and in succeeding chapters.

amateur	leisure
development	liaison
fulfill	privilege
immediately	transferred
itinerary	volume

Proofreading Tips

Study these tips and apply them as you proofread:

1. Punctuation marks are used in order to make the meaning clear. Proofread to eliminate confusion caused by errors in punctuation.

2. If the material is interesting, read first for pleasure, then for errors.

3. Keep a reference guide ready in case you need to refer to it.

10-7—10-8

Maine, have
10,000 shoes
12, 17

PROOFREADING APPLICATIONS

Proofread the following paragraphs and use the appropriate proofreading symbols to mark errors you find in terminal punctuation, comma usage, or spelling. To aid you in proofreading, the number of errors to be found is indicated in parentheses at the end of Exercises P-1, P-2, and P-3. You must find them on your own in Exercise P-4.

P-1 Do you routinely use an ATM (automatic teller machine) to withdraw money from your checking account? to transfer funds between accounts? to pay regular monthly bills? Many of us are no longer amaters at this form of electronic funds transfer, and find it a convenient flexible method of banking. Did you know that these services may be available even if you are thousands of miles from your bank's ATM. Many of the 60,000 ATMs in our country are linked into statewide, regional, or national networks. (4)

P-2 The small plastic card you use at your ATM is actually a debit card. It allows you to withdraw from your account electronically without ever writing a check. Would you like to be able to use your debit card right at the cash register? You would merely put your debit card through a processing machine, enter your personal code and depress a computer-entry button. The amount of your purchase would be immediatly deducted from your checking account, and transfered to the store's account. (4)

P-3 The developement of point-of-sale debiting has been slow, but this debiting method has the enthusiasm of many persons. Retailers get their money almost immediately, and chances of a hold-up are diminished because money is deposited in the store's account rather than into its cash register. Customers enjoy the priviledges of paying faster, carrying less cash, and not having to wait in line for check approval. Do you think banks will ever feel threatened that debit cards may cause them to lose their high-volume, profitable, credit card business. (4)

P-1

1. amateurs
2. transfer and
3. convenient, flexible
4. bank's ATM?

P-2

1. code, and
2. immediately
3. account and
4. transferred

CHAPTER 10—Proofreading for Punctuation Errors, Part 1

P-4 Would you like to receive current relevant information about our new All-in-One card. Just return the enclosed coupon to National Bank, 1987 Wilshire Boulevard, Los Angeles CA 90024-8765. Send in your coupon by February 15, 1987 and you will receive a rebate of 1 percent on all All-in-One credit purchases above the first $1000 in any 12-month period.

P-3

1. development
2. privileges
3. profitable credit
4. card business?

P-4

1. current, relevant
2. All-in-One card?
3. Los Angeles, CA
4. February 15, 1987,
5. $1,000

PROGRESSIVE PROOFREADING

The following section provides an opportunity for you to apply proofreading skills to a job situation:

You are the manager of McDowell Travel Agency. Since this is a relatively new business, only four people are employed in the office. You confer with customers and make travel reservations, but you are also responsible for seeing that all communication is correct. Today you have four documents to proofread. Follow the instructions given with each document. Your office uses the block letter style and open punctuation.

Job 1: Letter to a prospective customer.

Job 2: Personal Data Sheet.

Job 3: An information sheet that you have prepared for people interested in cruises.

Job 4: Copy of printed ad.

Job 1 Mark any errors you find.

McDowell Travel Agency

4500 West Kennedy Boulevard • Tampa, FL 33609-3421 • (800) 555-2435

October 25, 19--

Col. Edward C. Barrett
1100 Madison Ave.
Goldsboro, NC 27530-8959

Dear Col. Barrett

Thank you for your letter of October 15 requesting brochures,
price lists and information sheets about cruises leaving from
Miami, FL. Your inquiry comes at a time when there are a
number of interesting, exotic curises at fabulously low
prices.

I have requested that three cruise lines send you up-to-date
information about their winter cruises, and I am sure you
will hear from them soon. Consider each line's total cost
the cost of air travel to the point of departure, and the
itinerary when you are making a choice. You will note that
prices for a seven-day cruise range from $625 to $1800 per
person.

I have enclosed information about choosing a cruise that I
hope will be helpful. After you make your desicion about
the cruise, fill out and return the data sheet. You can
then leave everything in our hands and rest assured that
satisfactory arrangements will be made.

We look forward to serving as your laisison with the cruise
line of your choice and to assist you in any way possible.

Sincerely

Mrs. Laura E. Spellman
Marketing Manager

os

Job 2 Compare the typed copy and rough draft below, using appropriate proofreading symbols to correct any errors.

PERSONAL DATA SHEET

Name _____

Address _____

Spouse (if any) _____

Cruise No. _____

Destination _____

Departure Date _____

Return Date _____ (

Insurance Desired   Yes ____
                     No ____

~~Name of~~ Person to Call in Case of Emergency _____
_____   Telephone Number _____

FOR OFFICE USE ONLY:
LAST NAME
SHIP NO.
RECEIPT NO.

PERSONAL DATA SHEET

Name _____

Address _____

Spouse (if any) _____

Destenation _____

Departure Date _____

Return Date _____

Insurance Desired   Yes _____
                    No _____

Name of Person to Call in Case of Emergency _____
                    Telephone Number _____

FOR OFFICE USE ONLY: LAST NAME: _____
                       SHIP NO. _____   RECEIPT NO. _____

Job 3   Check this information sheet for errors. Be sure that all words are spelled correctly.

CHOOSING THE RIGHT CRUISE FOR YOU

As the winter cruise season approaches, discounts on ship fares are plentiful in the travel industry, and smart consumers are taking advantage of the special bargains. Now is the time to consider taking a liesurely cruise if it is one of those things that will fullfill a lifetime dream for you. If you have never pictured yourself as a passenger on a cruise ship, consider the facts given below.

Passenger Profile

Once cruises were a pastime for the rich and the retired. Today cruises are taken by individuals from all walks of life and all in-come levels. Forty-eight percent of cruise passengers now earn less than $25,000 a year. Nearly half are under forty-five years of age, and ten percent are under twenty-five.

It is estimated that more than a million and a half people will take cruises on about one hundred cruise ships this year and cruise lines are competitively vying for this business. Two qualities of the cruise experience is being stressed: value and convenience. Now is a great time to participate in what some refer to as the "cruise revolution.

Cost and Convenence

Consider the price of the average cruise. The price that you pay includes accomodations, baggage handling, meals, entertainment (including first-run movies and live performances), room service, daily activities ranging from computer lessons to disco dancing, travel to any number of ports, and reduced air fare from home.

Convenience is another factor that you must consider as you contemplate taking a cruise. In what other way can you travel from one country to another without having to unpack and repack your bags? Where else can you spend days or weeks without having to open your wallet or purse constantly? You don't even have to worry about arranging travel schedules, making plane reservations, or to wait long hours in airports.

Activities on Board

To be sure that your cruise proves to be all that you expect it to be, you should take the time to find out what the various cruise lines offer and to who they cater. For example, some cruise lines cater to children and make special provisions for them. Other lines cater only to adults. Some provide for academic pursuits while others primarily provide entertainment and recreation.

You should give some thought to the types of activities that you might enjoy. Do you want entertainment. Do you want some physical fitness programs? Do you want to learn something? There is at least one cruise ship that doubles on a regular basis as a floating university. There is no pressure to participate in any of the activities provided by the cruise line. If you wish, you can relax on the deck with a book or watch television in your own cabin. You can choose your own recreation.

Cruise Itinarary

Another important criteria that will effect your selection of a cruise is the planned itinarary of the ship. Consider the number of stops you would be making and the ports you would be visiting. Are there particular cities you have always wanted to tour.

Your travel agent can provide you with a detailed list of port choices and itinerary options to help you decide on the best cruise.

How to Get Started

After you have made some of the major decisions reguarding your preferences in a cruise, see your travel agent. The agent can help determine which cruise suits your needs, and provide answers to any other questions that you might have. In other words, your travel agent is the liason between you and the cruise line. Using a travel agent is the best way to take the worry out of traveling. Contact your travel agent today.

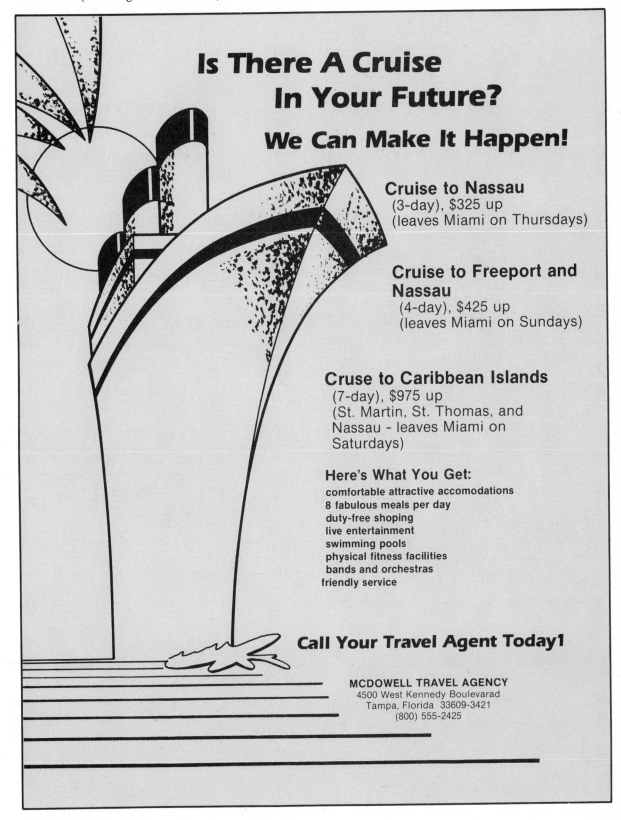

Chapter 11

Proofreading for Punctuation Errors, Part 2

Objectives: *After completing this chapter, you should be able to*

1. Identify errors in commas used to set off introductory elements, nonessential elements, appositives, nouns of direct address, and contrasted elements.
2. Use appropriate proofreading symbols to indicate changes in text.

Functions of the Comma

Chapter 10 dealt with terminal punctuation and some simple uses of the comma. Chapter 11 discusses the more complex uses of the comma. This chapter covers rules for using commas to (1) separate introductory elements from the rest of the sentence, (2) set off nonessential expressions, (3) set off appositives, and (4) set off nouns of direct address. Generally two commas are used to *set off* nonessential elements that interrupt the flow of thought from subject to verb or complement. One comma is used to *separate* elements in a sentence to clarify their relationship.

Introductory Elements

Introductory elements are words, phrases, or clauses that begin a sentence and come before the subject and verb of the main clause. Generally a single comma is used to separate an introductory element from the rest of the sentence in order to clarify the meaning of the sentence.

11-1 Use a comma after most introductory elements.

         S   V
Yes, we have up-to-date driving manuals.
    (introductory word)

S   V

Remember, the books must be returned today.
       (introductory word)

            S V

Having taken the message myself, I feel confident it is correct.
       (introductory phrase)

         S   V

To assemble the kit, you must follow the directions.
       (introductory phrase)

■ Do not mistake the main clause of the sentence for an introductory clause. A comma is not used when the main clause comes first.

                       S   V

After you have completed this assignment, you may take a 15-minute break.
        (introductory clause)

S   V

You may take a 15-minute break after you have completed this assignment.

■ Do not use a comma after phrases that function as the subject of the sentence even though they may look like simple introductory elements.

            S   V

Finding the lost contact lens is their goal.
     (noun phrase used as subject)

S   V

To accept sole credit for the idea would be unfair.
    (infinitive phrase used as subject)

11-2 Do not use a comma after *short* introductory phrases or introductory words that answer such questions as when, how often, where, or why.

In the morning things may look better.

Frequently the class visits the history museum.

Proofread the following sentences for errors in the use of the comma. Mark any errors, using the proofreading symbols you have learned thus far. If a sentence is correct, mark a *C* to the right of it.

a. When the fuel light comes on, you should begin looking for a service station.

b. Under the Gramm-Rudman Act an unemployed person is entitled to benefits.

c. Although the two leaders disagreed on some points, the meeting was beneficial.

d. Yes I am a member of Professional Secretaries International.

e. We will not go to school, if it snows.

Nonessential and Essential Elements

A nonessential element is a word, phrase, or clause that describes and can therefore be omitted without changing the basic meaning of the sentence. An essential element is one that is necessary to the meaning of the sentence. Nonessential elements are also referred to as nonrestrictive or parenthetical. Essential elements are also referred to as restrictive.

To determine whether an expression is essential or nonessential, try omitting it from the sentence. If you can leave the expression out without changing the meaning of the sentence, it is a nonessential expression and should be set off with commas.

11-1—11-2

a. C

b. Act͜an

c. C

d. Yes͜I

e. school͜if

11-3   Use commas to set off nonessential elements.

It is possible, *theoretically*, to make the experiment work.

We knew that, *late or not*, we were expected to attend that meeting.

The person who received the recognition, *if you recall*, was the supervisor.

Mr. Kemper, *who was recently hired as a biology instructor*, is looking for a house.

I am sorry I cannot give you Cabin No. 20, *which you occupied last week*.

- Do not use commas to set off elements that are essential to the meaning of the sentence.

The student *who studies hard and completes all the prepsheets* should make a good grade.

All orders *that are postmarked by December 6* will be shipped before Christmas.

11-4 Use commas to set off such transitional expressions as *on the other hand, first, in fact, to tell the truth, however, that is, then, therefore,* and *for example* when they interrupt or change the flow of the sentence.

She may, *however,* choose to spend the extra time watching a television special.

You could, *on the other hand,* refuse to accompany her.

 Proofread the following sentences for errors in the use of the comma. Mark any errors, using the proofreading symbols you have learned thus far. If a sentence is correct, mark a *C* to the right of it.

a. The statements highlighted in yellow are important in this course.

b. The woman, who is standing by the punch table, is my wife.

c. Leisure activities, which include swimming and sailing are important to me.

d. She has not been to church since she returned home.

e. He was unfortunately a victim of depression.

Appositives

An *appositive* is a word or phrase that renames or can be substituted for the noun or pronoun that it follows. An appositive makes the meaning clearer, but the main thought of the sentence normally would not be affected if the appositive were omitted.

11-5 Use commas to set off appositives.

The scoutmaster, *Mr. Scobee,* is planning a camping trip to Arlington.

11-3—11-4

a. C
b. woman who
   table is
c. sailing, are
d. C
e. was, unfortunately,

Theresa Fowlkes, *a benefits consultant with Higgins Co.*, reported that only a small percentage of companies allow unused vacation time to accrue.

■ Do not use commas to set off an appositive when it contains information that is essential to the meaning of the sentence or has a close relationship to the preceding word.

Her daughter *Barbara* is going on vacation.
(She has more than one daughter; Barbara is the one who is going on vacation.)
The doctor *himself* did the testing.

 Proofread the following sentences for errors in the use of the comma. Mark any errors, using the proofreading symbols you have learned thus far. If a sentence is correct, mark a *C* to the right of it.

   a. Her latest book, *Meeting the Challenge*, was a big hit.

   b. Mr. George McAbee, chairman of the department, is going to conduct the seminar.

   c. Have the materials delivered to Marjorie the chauffeur.

   d. According to Jim Clark of Clark Associates producers of on-line directory services, over half of the data bases provide business-related information.

   e. The author herself was there to autograph the books.

Additional Comma Rules

The following guidelines are to help you use the comma correctly in special situations. Rules for direct address and contrasted elements are discussed along with guidelines for the use of the comma to prevent misreading.

11-5
a. C
b. C
c. Marjorie, the
d. Associates, producers
e. C

11-6 Use a comma to set off a name or title addressed directly to the reader or listener.

I cannot locate an error on this page, *Dr. Dellasaga*.

Ask the participants, *Ms. Templeton*, if they are planning to stay for lunch.

11-7 Use a comma to set off contrasted elements.

> The president, *not the board*, made the decision.
>
> John, *rather than Paul*, will make the presentation.

■ When a contrasted element is considered essential to the meaning of the sentence, it is not set off by commas.

> It was a busy but enjoyable trip.

11-8 Insert a comma to prevent misreading the sentence.

> *Confusing:* Inside the house was a mess.
>
> *Better:* Inside, the house was a mess.
>
> *Confusing:* To Joe Alexander seemed the man for the job.
>
> *Better:* To Joe, Alexander seemed the man for the job.

Note: Use this rule sparingly. Generally *all* commas are inserted to make reading easier.

11-9 Insert a comma to separate identical or similar words, except when the addition of a comma would increase the awkwardness of the sentence.

> They walked in, in groups.
>
> He felt that that statement was not in good taste.

■ Insert a comma to separate unrelated numbers that fall next to each other.

> In 1986, 800 people attended the city's annual fair.

Proofread the following sentences for errors in the use of the comma. Mark any errors, using the proofreading symbols you have learned thus far. If a sentence is correct, mark a *C* to the right of it.

a. I believe Miss Burt that your order has been received.

b. Out of three, one choice was possible.

c. To a perfectionist like Joan Marie would not be acceptable for the assignment.

d. The personal computer not the typewriter is my choice.

e. I am happy Caroline received the promotion.

Spelling Review

To improve your ability to detect spelling errors, master the words below. Watch for them in the exercises that follow and in succeeding chapters.

appropriate	occurrence
conscientious	questionnaire
convenience	receipt
facilitate	strictly
integrate	utilization

Proofreading Tips

Study these tips and apply them as you proofread:

1. When proofreading for comma errors, always look for the main thought in the sentence and determine if the main thought is changed by the use of commas. Do not use commas to set off material that is essential to the meaning.

2. Remember, only one comma is needed to set off an introductory word, phrase, or clause.

3. Two commas are required to set off words, phrases, or clauses within a sentence.

11-6—11-9

a. believe, Miss Burt, that
b. C
c. Joan, Marie
d. computer, not the typewriter, is
e. C

PROOFREADING APPLICATIONS

Proofread the following paragraphs and use the appropriate proofreading symbols to mark errors you find in spelling and the use of the comma. To aid you in proofreading, the number of errors to be found is indicated in parentheses at the end of Exercises P-1, P-2, and P-3. You must find them on your own in Exercise P-4.

P-1 According to research, health is not threatened by radiation from video display terminals (VDTs). However blurry vision, burning, and tearing are common complaints. Factors, such as glare and poor contrast between the display's background and the images, cause eyestrain. To reduce eyestrain, keyboards, displays, and chairs that are adjustable should be used. Additionally a 15-minute break should be taken for every two hours of work at a VDT. Concern for the health of operators continues to be widespread. In fact many states have passed laws regulating working conditions for operators. (5)

P-2 Conscientous word processing specialists realize that proofreading is critical to producing quality communications even though it requires intense concentration on the display. Effective utilization of the features of the word processing system, however, can reduce the time spent viewing the screen and consequently reduce eyestrain. Use of the search feature to locate text within a document, for example, will eliminate the procedure of manually scrolling through the entire document. Likewise use of the search-and-replace feature to locate and replace repetitive errors in the text is faster than correcting each occurence of an error through a lengthy time-consuming procedure. (5)

P-3 Ms. Spiegel, the manager of word processing services made several suggestions that have benefited both the word processing specialists and the originators. To reduce unnecessary keystrokes and proofreading, she suggested that frequently used letters be prepared as standard text. When form letters are requested only the variables have to be keyed and proofread. Ms. Spiegel also advised the specialists to

P-1

1. However, blurry
2. Factors such as
3. images cause
4. Additionally,
5. In fact, many

P-2

1. Conscientious
2. and, consequently,
3. Likewise, use
4. occurrence
5. lengthy, time-consuming

utilize the dictionary/spelling software which is helpful for locating keyboarding errors. As well as decreasing spelling errors in the final document, this software lessens the time required for proofreading. (3)

P-4 Diane Gilbert, director of word processing for the American Bar Association in Chicago suggests that occasionally it may be appropirate to proofread documents after they have been printed rather than before. When documents are wider than the display for example, the operator must horizontally scroll through the text. The left side of the text moves off the display, as the right side moves on. To compare both sides of the document, the operator must rely stricly on visual memory. This is difficult, especially if the text is of a statistical nature. Convenence to the operator and effective results, therefore, should be the criteria when deciding whether to proofread from hard copy or from the display.

PROGRESSIVE PROOFREADING

The following section provides an opportunity for you to apply your proofreading skills to a job situation:

You are employed as an editorial assistant for The Jackson Herald, a daily newspaper. You have the responsibility of proofreading the work of new reporters, and from time to time the chief editor asks you to proofread specific items. Here are the items that you are responsible for today:

Job 1: An article about desktop publishing that will appear in Sunday's paper.

Job 2: A report based on the experience and opinions of users of desktop publishing.

Job 3: An ad for software to be used for desktop publishing.

Job 1 Proofread the following article on desktop publishing.

The Jackson Herald

DESKTOP PUBLISHING

A New Concept in Document Production

What is destop publishing? Why is it capturing the attention of so many people? Will it revolutionize the appearance of documents? Will it become the standard way to produce ads and brochures? to produce all corporate communications?

Although some of these questions may remain unanswered for some time one thing is sure: Desktop publishing is definately changing the communication process for a number of organizations.

What Is Desktop Publishing?

Desktop publishing describes the process by which a professional quality document is produced using a microcomputer system and a special software. It thus enables the production of typeset-quality pages in-house.

IS WYSIWYG FOR YOU?

Software

WYSIWIG which stands for "What you see is what you get" characterizes much of the composition software. WYSIWYG (pronounced "wissy wig") means that what you see on the screen is exactly what you'll get when the copy is printed. Headlines appear in large and bold type, italics appear slanted, and vertical spacing appears as it will when printed.

Copy can be spread between columns on a page and multiple headings being used on a page.

Printer

Although a dot matrix printer can be utalized, laser printers facilatate the use of multiple type sizes and styles on the same page. Graphics such as letterheads and logos, free-hand drawings (done with a mouse), and scanned images such as photographs or drawings may be intergrated with copy.

"Desktop publishing may replace word processing software for final output."

Is There a Market?

Yesterday's "paperless" office is becoming today's "paperful office. Experts tell us that the average office worker had to read 900 pages of hard copy per month last year, and this figure is increasing by ten to fifteen percent each year. Utilzation of paper as the major means of communicating is likely to be with us for a long time.

Traditionally, offices have depended upon two types of paper communications: (1) typewriter output and (2) typeset output. Until recently, professional-quality printing was limited to the domain of graphic arts professionals: typesetters, pasteup artists, and printers Desktop publishing enables typeset-quality pages to be produced in-house. With a little practice, and some good design ideas, managers, office workers, or students can create their own layouts complete with borders, rules, columns of type and other graphic elements.

How Is It Used?

As shown from a questionaire sent to over ninty users, people are using desktop systems for an array of different purposes: ads, broshures, business forms, manuals, proposals, newsletters, resumes, and transparency masters.

Ms. Julie Newton vice president of a publishing consulting firm predicts that desktop publishing will even replace word processing software for final output. One consultant commented "Once you start producing professional looking pages, your audience will get used to it."

The potential of desktop publishing remains to be seen. Certainly it is providing a likable alternative to using outside typesetters for business publications.

"Once you start producing professional looking pages, your audience will get used to it."

This handout on desktop publishing was prepared by Kim Stephens. For more information on desktop publishing systems call her at Extension 212.

Job 2 Proofread the report below.

DOES DESKTOP PUBLISHING PAY?
HERE'S WHAT THEY SAY

The expansion of desktop publishing is now a certainty. Today's decision makers would do well to stop, look and listen to what users of desktop publishing systems are saying.

If "time is money" consider the money that can be saved by elimanating the turnaround time involved in producing documents through outside suppliers. A national car rental agency enjoyed increased revenues of 10% to 12% because it was able to produce price lists weekly in-house as compared to every three weeks using an outside source. Time was saved, and price lists were current.

A San Francisco photographer whom was relocating to New York designed and produced personal letterhead stationary and appropirate business cards in three hours using his computer.

Ambitious students are using there desktop systems to produce term papers. Consequently students who do not have excess to com-position software are complaining that there at a disadvantage. Some professors have ruled that, while neatness counts, typeset term papers are just a little _too_ neat.

An editor in charge of creating a 250-page software manual wanted it to appear typeset. The estimates for an outside typesetter and printer was approximately $10,000. She was able to purchase an entire system (computer, software, and printer) for slightly more than the printing costs of this one job.

Paul Brainerd, developer of the Page-Maker program, stated that publishing has come full circle. After Gutenberg, the publisher was also the printer--right in his own shop. Now the publisher can once again do the printing on his desktop.

Proofreading for Punctuation Errors, Part 3

Objectives: *After completing this chapter, you should be able to*

1. Detect errors in the use of these punctuation marks: semicolon, colon, apostrophe, quotation marks, underscore, dash, and parentheses.
2. Use appropriate proofreading symbols to indicate changes in text.

Punctuation to Clarify

As discussed in the last two chapters, marks of punctuation have specific, prescribed functions. Punctuation helps the reader to interpret the meaning of the communication. The proofreader must know the function of each mark of punctuation to be able to evaluate its use in clarifying the message.

Chapter 12 reviews the use of the semicolon, colon, apostrophe, quotation marks, underscore, dash, and parentheses. Use the following proofreading symbols to mark errors in the use of these punctuation marks.

/;\   Insert semicolon.

```
Fasten your seatbelts;we're ready
for takeoff.
```

/:\   Insert colon.

```
You will need to bring three things:
notepaper, pencil, and eraser.
```

\'/   Insert apostrophe or
        single quotation mark.

```
Tennessee's economic climate is con-
tinually improving.
```

　　　　　\\"　　　　　Insert quotation marks.

"When interest rates are down, invest
in stocks,/ advised the broker.

　　　　___ or ital　Underline or italicize.

The word _parallel_ should be included
in the list.

　　　　--/　　　　　Insert dash.

The thief took everything/my car,
my wallet, and my luggage.

　　　　(/)/　　　　Insert parentheses.

The committee/consisting of five
students and three teachers/presented
the report on time.

Semicolon

A semicolon is used when a sentence needs a stronger break than
would be provided by a comma. The semicolon is not as abrupt as a
period and does not signal the end of a thought as a period does. It is
a strong separator and is used only between equal parts. A semicolon
is followed by one space.

12-1　Use a semicolon to separate the main clauses of a compound
sentence when the clauses are not joined by a coordinate conjunction
(*and, but, or,* and *nor*).

I must go to vote; the polls will close in an hour.

Send the report by Federal Express Mail; we need an answer
tomorrow.
　　　(*You* is the understood subject in the first clause.)

12-2　Use a semicolon to separate the main clauses of a compound
sentence when either of the clauses contains a comma. Confusion
could occur if a comma were used to separate the clauses.

When you receive the document, sign it; but do not mail it until Friday, March 10.

I requested files for Carlson, Carson, and Davison; but files for Carlsen, Carson, and Davidson were delivered.

12-3   Use the semicolon to separate the main clauses of a compound sentence joined by an adverb or transitional expression such as *accordingly, consequently, furthermore, hence, however, in fact, likewise, otherwise, therefore,* and *thus.*

It was past midnight; consequently, they had to adjourn before the issue was settled.

The cost was minimal; however, he chose not to attend the meeting.

12-4   Use the semicolon to separate items in a series when at least one of the items contains a comma.

Copies of the report were sent to Elaine Carson, president; Janet Wukman, vice president; and Trilby Mays, secretary.

  Proofread the following sentences for errors in the use of commas and semicolons. If a sentence is correct, write a *C* to the right ot it.

    a. There was much disagreement on the issue, nevertheless the plan was finally approved.

    b. I will carry only the essentials, the nonessentials require too much space.

    c. I like to visit North Carolina, South Carolina and Georgia but Florida, Alabama, and Louisiana will be my destination this year.

    d. I detest dieting; it takes too much willpower.

    e. Imperial Airlines serves Miami, Florida, Atlanta, Georgia, Birmingham, Alabama, and Raleigh, North Carolina.

Colon

A colon represents a break in the sentence that is greater than the semicolon but less than the period. Usually the writer uses the colon after a statement to introduce and emphasize what follows the colon. The colon usually means *as follows*. Two spaces follow a colon except in expressions of time and reference initials.

12-5 Use a colon to introduce a question, a lengthy quotation, or a phrase or clause that explains what has gone before. The first word of a main clause following a colon may be capitalized for emphasis.

The speaker raised an interesting question: Which comes first, enthusiasm or success?

The researcher made these recommendations:

> (long quote)

Watson's philosophy was simple: Give the best service, strive for superior performance, and respect the individual.

12-6 Use a colon to introduce a list or a series. (Omit periods after items in a vertical list unless one or more of the items are complete sentences.)

> The steps are as follows:
> 1. Insert the disk into Drive 1.
> 2. Turn on the computer.
>
> These criteria are considered important:
> 1. A quality education
> 2. Meaningful work experience
> 3. Academic grade point average
> 4. Leadership experience

■ Do not use a colon to introduce a list that immediately follows a preposition or a verb.

The supervisor has the responsibility to (1) assist the staff, (2) establish procedures, and (3) resolve conflicts.

12-7 Use a colon to separate hours and minutes expressed in figures.

> Dinner will be served at 5:30 p.m.

·12-1—12-4

a. issue, nevertheless, the

b. essentials, the

c. South Carolina, and Georgia, but

d. C

e. Florida, Atlanta, Georgia, Birmingham, Alabama, and

12-8   Use a colon to punctuate reference initials in a letter or the salutation when mixed punctuation is used.

JP:df
Dear Ms. Fine:

 Proofread the following sentences for errors in the use of commas, semicolons, and colons. If a sentence is correct, write a *C* to the right of it.

a. Remember this proofreading tip: Always proofread a letter carefully before printing it.

b. The questionnaire included three sections; personal information, job information, and references.

c. The "Employment Policies" section of the *Policy Manual* states: "Spouses will not be permitted to continue their employment when one of them occupies a confidential position."

d. The article was sent to the following newspapers: *The News and Observer*, Raleigh, *The Bethel Beacon*, Bethel, and *The Daily Southern*, Tarboro.

e. In one hour I plan to do the following; spin the barrel of entries, draw ten slips from the barrel, and announce the winners.

Apostrophe

An apostrophe is used to form possessives and some plurals. It is also used to indicate the omission of letters and figures. The apostrophe is followed by a single space unless the next character is part of the same word.

12-9   Use an apostrophe and *s* to form the possessive case of singular nouns.

man's friend	(friend of man)
a year's work	(the work of a year)
Michael's hat	(the hat of Michael)

12-5—12-8

a. C
b. sections: personal
c. C
d. Raleigh; Bethel; and
e. following: spin

Note: The possessive case for some nouns is formed by adding only an apostrophe. Addition of an apostrophe and an *s* makes the word too difficult to pronounce.

> for appearance' (conscience', goodness', old times') sake
> species' habits

12-10 Use an apostrophe and *s* to form the possessive case of indefinite pronouns.

> anyone's guess
> everybody's friend
> somebody's glove

Note: Personal pronouns do not require an apostrophe.

> my/mine   our/ours
> your/yours their/theirs
> her/hers   its
> his

> This notebook is mine; yours is on the desk.

> The building has exceeded its capacity.

12-11 Use an apostrophe alone to form the possessive case of plural nouns ending in *s* or *es*.

> employees' rights   (rights of the employees)
> three years' work   (the work of three years)
> Davises' house   (house of the Davises)

■ Use an apostrophe and *s* to form the possessive case of nouns that do not form their plural by adding *s* or *es*.

> children's field trip (field trip of the children)
> men's coats   (coats of the men)
> women's coats   (coats of the women)

12-12 To form the possessive of compound nouns, make the last element possessive.
daughter-in-law's schedule (the schedule of my daughter-in-law)
daughters-in-laws' schedules (the schedules of my daughters-in-law)
somebody else's

12-13 To show joint ownership, make the last name possessive. To show separate ownership, make each name possessive.

Marvin and Joyce's condominium (one condominium owned by both)
Brian's and Ben's rackets (two rackets, one Brian's and one Ben's)

12-14 Use an apostrophe to form the plural of letters, abbreviations containing periods, and words which would otherwise be confusing if only an *s* were added.

> B.A.'s
> A's and S's
> &'s (ampersands)

12-15 Use an apostrophe to indicate the omission of letters or figures.

> OK'd (okayed)
> it's (it is)
> o'clock (of the clock)
> class of '89 (class of 1989)

 Proofread the following sentences for errors in the use of the apostrophe. If a sentence is correct, write a *C* to the right of it.

a. The CPA decided to analyze the investor's balance sheet.

b. The records filed in Margaret's and Bob's bankruptcy case revealed errors in the hundreds of dollars.

c. For old times sake, let's celebrate Louise's and Frank's anniversary with flowers.

d. Its a good idea to check the company's letterhead for proper spelling, punctuation, and use of abbreviations such as ampersands (&'s).

e. Her complaint was that there were too many *ands* in the students' essay and that there was a noticeable repetition of *moreover's*.

Quotation Marks

Quotation marks are used to enclose words quoted (spoken or written), titles, or words used in an unusual manner. Generally use a comma to set off a quotation.

12-16   Use quotation marks to enclose a direct quotation.

Jim Goes said, "I expect attendance to be good at our next AMS meeting."

"All correspondence should be answered," said the manager, "within two days."

Was it Evelyn who said, "The meeting is now adjourned"?

Note: Place a question mark outside the quotation marks if the entire statement is a question. Place the question mark inside the quotation marks if only the quoted material is a question. Place commas and periods inside quotation marks.

Gary asked, "Is it time to leave?"

12-17   Use single quotation marks to enclose a quotation within a quotation.

In his speech to the graduating class, Dean Stanhope remarked, "I believe that, as John Kennedy said, 'It is time for a new generation of leadership . . . for there is a new world to be won.' "

12-18   Use quotation marks to enclose titles of book chapters, articles in magazines or newspapers, or other parts of complete works. (Underscore titles of books, magazines, newspapers, or other complete works.)

One of the most popular columns in the *News and Observer* is "Under the Dome."

The article "Microimage Methods" in the April issue of *Administrative Management* provides an analysis of the film and electronic technologies.

12-19   Use quotation marks to enclose words or expressions that are used in a special manner or that may be unfamiliar to the reader. This technique should be used sparingly lest it lose its effectiveness.

Wohl stated that many companies have "Adidas networks" in which you run the diskette down the hall to your co-worker.

"Computer phobia" is causing many managers to communicate poorly with the consultants.

The Underscore

The underscore is used to give special emphasis to certain words or expressions. In typewritten copy, italics are indicated by underscoring. A printer sets all underscored words in italic type.

12-20   Use the underscore to set off titles of published works including books, magazines, newspapers, and video tape recordings. Also underline plays, movies, television series, and musical compositions.

We rented the videotape *Sound of Music* and thoroughly enjoyed watching it.

Our library subscribes to *The Wall Street Journal* and numerous periodicals, including *Modern Office Technology* and *Personal Computing*.

12-21   Use the underscore to set off words being emphasized, defined, or used as examples. Foreign words should be underscored if they are likely to be unfamiliar to the reader.

Successful managers are *leaders*—not bosses.

They traveled *à pied* (on foot) to the Eiffel Tower.

Glower means "to look with sullen annoyance or anger."

For example, *imminent* should be included in the appendix with other confusing words.

■   Use the underscore to refer to a word or letter.

I think we should delete *the* from the sentence.

He added an *s* to my name.

Proofread the following sentences for errors in the use of quotation marks and the underscore. If a sentence is correct, write a *C* to the right of it.

a. John said, "The emphasis of the advertisement should be *voluntary* participation.

b. Optical disks were discussed in the article Magnetic Media Still Tops in WP-OA Storage, which appeared in the February issue of *Office Systems*.

c. Sally asked, 'Did you go to the movie last night"?

d. The flight attendant asked, "Are you concerned about your safety on this flight?"

e. You are lying, "n'est-ce pas"?

The Dash

12-16—12-21

The dash, an informal mark of punctuation, is used to indicate a sudden change in thought and to emphasize what follows. Use the dash sparingly so that it does not lose its impact. No space precedes or follows the dash.

a. participation."
b. "Magnetic . . . Storage,"
c. "Did . . . night?"
d. C
e. <u>n'est-ce pas</u>

12-22   Use a dash to indicate a sudden change in thought.

The best way—perhaps the only way—is to work overtime the next two weeks.

The political impact of his action—and that's what counts—cannot be measured.

12-23   Use a dash in place of commas to set off a nonessential element that needs special emphasis.

That man is a thief—and I can prove it!

Successful organizations have a common source of power—people.

■   Use a dash in place of a semicolon for a stronger but less formal break between two independent clauses in a sentence.

Frequently when people get upset, they don't expect you to provide answers—they just need to unleash their feelings.

■ Use a dash in place of a colon to introduce explanatory words, phrases, or clauses when a stronger but less formal break is desired.

Within two hours we had experienced a variety of weather—hail, rain, sunshine.

To obtain the money, Jeff had to sell everything—his car, his house, and all of his furniture.

The Parentheses

Parentheses are used to enclose nonessential, supplementary, or illustrative information. Unlike dashes, parentheses de-emphasize information.

12-24   Use parentheses to separate nonessential information from the rest of the sentence.

To obtain your complimentary pass, stop at the second ticket booth (the one with the red flag on it).

12-25   Use parentheses to explain an abbreviation or to enclose periods of time.

An immediate 10 percent salary increase will be given to any person with a CPS (Certified Professional Secretary) rating.

The latter part of the twentieth century (1987-2000) will be a period of spectacular growth and change.

12-26   Use parentheses to enclose characters in a run-in enumeration.

To enter the contest, you must (1) fill in the application form, (2) pay an entry fee, and (3) mail your entry.

Proofread the following sentences for errors in the use of the dash and parentheses.

a. The curriculum was presented at the OSRA (Office Systems Research Association) convention held in March.

b. An article in yesterday's paper—or was it today's—gave the pairings for the tournament.

c. Managing a company keeping it growing, profitable, and abreast of technology is a giant balancing act.

d. Spending for leisure products (from skateboards to compact-disk players) has doubled over the past ten years.

e. Please use the side entrance—the one on Arlington Boulevard.

Spelling Review

To improve your ability to detect spelling errors, master the words below. Watch for them in the exercises that follow and in succeeding chapters.

achievement	noticeable
analysis	parallel
bankruptcy	permissible
debtor	repetition
explanation	undoubtedly

Proofreading Tips

Study these tips and apply them as you proofread:

1. Check each sentence to be sure a closing parenthesis, dash, or quotation mark has not been omitted.

2. Check to be sure that punctuation marks convey the proper meaning. Query the originator if necessary.

3. Check to be sure that substitutions have been entered where words have been crossed out.

4. Proofread each document twice—once for mechanical errors and once for content errors.

12-22—12-26
a. C
b. C
c. company—keeping technology—is
d. C
e. entrance (the Boulevard).

PROOFREADING APPLICATIONS

Proofread the following paragraphs and use appropriate proofreading symbols to mark errors you find in punctuation and spelling. To aid you in proofreading, the number of errors to be found is indicated in parentheses at the end of exercises P-1, P-2, and P-3. You must find them on your own in exercise P-4.

P-1   Although we strive a lifetime to achieve success, will we recognize it when we reach it? What is success? How do we measure it? Undoubtly, rewards, recognition, and promotions are all important in determining success, however, we must also measure our acheivements by our own standards. For some people this means knowing their performance is more than just *muddling through* every day. To others, success may involve giving a quality performance each day. To still others, success may not be job related at all. It could mean bringing out the best in at least one other person. (5)

P-2   In her keynote address, Dr. Joyce Brothers made the following statement: "It is no exaggeration that a good self-image is the best possible preparation for success in life. Self-confidence affects every aspect of human behavior: the ability to learn; the capacity to grow and change; the choice of friends, mates, and careers." Equipped with a strong self-image, people expect to succeed. They believe in themselves act on their own strengths and in the final analsys, do not consider anything but a quality performance permassable. (4)

P-3   An article by Allan Cox summarized his philosophy of success in a recent issue of Management World. His philosophy is treated more extensively in his book *The Making of an Achiever*. According to Cox, "Achievers have no magical secrets; they simply recognize how to be the best persons possible and strive to meet the challenge." In meeting

P-1

1. Undoubtedly
2. success; however
3. achievements
4. "muddling through"

P-2

1. themselves, act
2. strengths, and
3. analysis
4. permissible

challenges, the achiever—through the repitition of his or her actions—encourages others to do the same. Cox states that achievers have four main attributes; they are other-centered, courageous, judicious, and resourceful. Of these attributes, focusing on others showing and being shown acceptance is perhaps the most important. (4)

P-4 Today's organizations are responding to the shift in employees attitudes towards compensation—from compensation purely as a means of survival to compensation as a means of gaining various personal benefits. One organizational approach is to offer a *cafeteria of compensation*, which allows employees to choose their own combination of salary, pension, and benefits. Other companies provide in-house fitness centers, child care, and student loans and scholarships. To nurture a managers commitment, some companies are devising salary systems based on what a manager "can" do and on the managers knowledge, rather than on performance alone. These innovative plans are helping organizations match their employee's values with reward systems.

P-3
1. <u>Management World</u>
2. repetition
3. attributes:
4. (showing . . . acceptance)

P-4
1. employees' attitudes
2. "cafeteria of compensation"
3. manager's commitment
4. manager <u>can</u> do
5. manager's knowledge rather
6. employees' values

PROGRESSIVE PROOFREADING

The following section provides an opportunity for you to apply your proofreading skills to a job situation:

The Maryland Farm Association is an active organization, and your responsibilities touch all of its functions. Officially, you are a secretary to the president but you also work closely with the editor of the organization's publication, *The Maryland Farm News*. Proofread the following documents for errors in spelling, grammatical construction, punctuation, number usage, and format. Your office uses the block letter style with open punctuation.

Job 1: A memorandum from the president to Farm Association members.

Job 2: A letter to a national figure who is being asked to speak at the Farm Association convention.

Job 3: An article for the publication.

Job 1 Proofread the memorandum below.

Maryland Farm Association

1920 Sherwood Road   Baltimore, MD 21227-5057

TO: Farm Association Members

FROM: Tim Jenkins, President

DATE: April 10, 19--

SUBJECT: Membership Renewal

No one knows the needs of the farmer better than the farmer.
Through the years, the Farm Association has been the voice of
farmers from coast to coast.

The Farm Association continues to be an influential voice for
agriculture. The Associations' passed record in legislatures nationwide is evidence of this influence: Thirty farm bills were
introduced in state legislatures within the last year.

The achievments of the Association is due to policy developements
at the local, state, and national level. The most noticable
strength of the organization is at the local level, because thats
where policies originate and action begins.

With the number of farmers decreasing each year, we must exert
extra effort to retain existing members by strengthening involvement, particularly at the local level. Paralelling this effort,
we must strive to enroll new members.

Show your commitment to the success of agriculture by following
these steps--1- fill in the membership renewal form, -2- attach
your check for $25 and -3- dropping your letter in the mailbox.
It could be--and probably will be--the best investment you will
ever make.

sf

Maryland Farm Association

1920 Sherwood Road   Baltimore, MD 21227-5057

Mr. Clifton Everett, President
Iowa Farm Assoication
689 Hazel Street
Boise, IO 83702-3782

Dear Mr. Everett

When the Planning Committee for the Maryland Farm Association, MFA,
State Convention met to plan next years convention, you were unami-
mously chosen to be the keynote speaker. We hope you will be able
to accept our invitation--and this is your invitation--to be with us.

The MFA Convention is scheduled for November 17-19 at the Radisson
Hotel in Baltimore, your presentation would be at 10 a.m. on
November 18.

Our members are extremely concerned about the increasing number of
bankrupcies, 72 in our state this year. We would like you to share
your analsis of the recent legislation, that is having a crucial
affect upon farmers, and outline a plan for financial farm management.
Please mention strategies for handling debtor obligations prudently.
You could (for example) outline the financial assistants available
to farmers, however, you may choose your own topic. Members who
have heard you speak report that your explantions are extremely
clear and your delivery is superb.

If you agree to be our keynote speaker on November 18, we will pay
you an honorarium of $200.00, and we will pay travel, meal, and
lodging expenses. Please let us know within 2 weeks whether you
can be our speaker.

Sincerely

Corey B. Dupree
State Convetnion Committee

sf

Job 3 Check the following news article for errors.

WHAT IS HAPPENING TO RURAL AMERICA?

To city dwellers, the word <u>rural</u> brings certain things to mind, rolling hills and picturesque barns, pickup trucks and loaded hay wagons, limited employment opportunities, and a population on the decline. On the contrary, rural America is changing. The population involved in agriculture-related businesses are growing.

A report prepared by the Dept. of Ag. analyzed 2,443 nonmetropolitan counties--those that make up rural America--and found that the population has increased over a 10-year period by 16 percent-- nearly twice the rate of metroplitan countries.

Out of a total of 2,442 702 (less than 29 percent) of the nonmetropolitan counties are dominated by farming. Consider the fact that only one out of every forty people today actually lives on the farm. 55 years ago one fourth of Americans lived on farms.

One might naturally ask, "Why then is the population of rural America growing?" Today there are many more individuals engaged in getting farm products to the consumer. They include farm suppliers, transportation workers, wholesalers and retailers; chefs, waiters, and waitresses; and cashiers and office workers engaged in these businesses.

Including those individuals engaged in providing products and services that are farm-related, U. S. agriculture employs about 23 million people. These individuals supply the 714 meals (and snacks) that are consumed in the U. S. each day--a <u>gastronomical</u> figure!

Although the number of Americans living on farms today has decreased, more Americans than ever before are closely associated with rural America. Rural America is still making an impact that is felt across the nation.

Chapter 13

Proofreading for Capitalization Errors

Objectives: *After completing this chapter, you should be able to*

1. Recognize capitalization errors.
2. Use appropriate proofreading symbols to indicate changes in text.

Functions of Capitalization

Capitalization gives distinction, emphasis, and importance to words. Words may be capitalized in one instance and not in another, depending on the relative importance the writer wishes to attach to them. The current preference is not to overuse capitalization in business writing. Emphasis is lost when too many words are capitalized. If your workplace has special rules for the use of capitals, follow its style guide.

Use the following symbols to indicate changes in capitalization:

Cap or ≡   Use a capital letter.

Computer science 2112
         ≡

lc or /   Use a lowercase letter.

My /Dear Mrs. Billings

General Guidelines

The following are general principles for the capitalization of words. Your proofreading accuracy should improve as these rules are reviewed.

13-1 Capitalize the first word of a sentence, a question, or a direct quotation.

Exercise every day.

When did the meeting adjourn?

The memo read, "Revised guidelines are in effect immediately."

■ Capitalize a phrase or a single word that expresses a complete thought.

Not now? Why?

13-2 Capitalize the first word of each item in a displayed list or an outline.

Order the following supplies:

Paper

Envelopes

Staples

13-3 Capitalize the first word after a colon if that word begins a complete sentence.

I had a surprise: My friends gave me a birthday party.

She had one purpose in mind: to get the job.

 Proofread the following sentences for capitalization errors. If a sentence is correct, write a *C* to the right of it.

a. Valerie asked, "have you ordered the supplies?"

b. David is concerned about one thing: Finishing the job.

c. The question on everyone's mind is this: who will be the next manager?

d. I can offer you the following beverages:
   1. milk
   2. juice
   3. water

e. did you cancel your vacation plans?

13-4 Capitalize the first word and all important words in titles and headings. Do not capitalize articles (*a, an, the*), conjunctions (*and, but, nor, or*), and prepositions (*in, for, of, with*) unless they are the first or last words.

Book: Information Processing for the Electronic Office
Magazine: The Saturday Evening Post

Newspaper: *The Wilmington Morning Star*

    Article: "How to Dress for Success"

Seminar: "How to Give Effective Performance Appraisals"

Proofread the following sentences for capitalization errors. If a sentence is correct, write a *C* to the right of it.

  a. Have you read the article, "Career Jobs for new College Grads"?

  b. Betsy's latest book is *Information Processing for the 1990s.*

  c. Did you see this month's issue of *The Journal of The Arts*?

  d. The movie *Out Of Africa* received many Oscar nominations.

  e. I read about the Dogwood Festival in *The Knoxville News-Sentinel.*

Proper Nouns

As a general guideline, capitalize proper nouns or names of specific persons, places, and things. Following are some rules to help you in determining when a noun should be capitalized.

13-5 Capitalize proper nouns as well as the personal pronoun *I*. Do not capitalize common nouns that do not refer to a specific person, place, or thing.

Colorado River	*but* the river
University of Tennessee	*but* the university
Advanced Algebra 3076	*but* advanced algebra
Billings Chamber of Commerce	*but* chamber of commerce

13-6 Capitalize well-known descriptive names or nicknames that are used to designate particular people, places, or things.

    the First Lady
    Babe Ruth (George Herman Ruth)

13-1—13-3

a. <u>have you</u>

b. F́inishing

c. <u>who</u>

d. 1. <u>milk</u>

   2. <u>juice</u>

   3. <u>water</u>

e. <u>did you</u>

13-4

a. **New**

b. C

c. *of the Arts?*

d. *Out of*

e. C

13-7   Capitalize words derived from proper names.

Texan   American

Note: Some derivatives change to common adjectives through frequent use.

french fries   plaster of paris
roman numerals   china dishes

Proofread the following sentences for capitalization errors. If a sentence is correct, write a *C* to the right of it.

a. Marilyn Cole is a member of the Future business leaders of America.

b. On her way to Denver, Colorado, she saw the Mississippi river for the first time.

c. Appropriately enough, she visited the Truman library in Independence, Missouri, on Friday, July 4.

d. We traveled through the Sunflower State on our way from Oklahoma to Nebraska.

e. Her first meal in Colorado was at a Mexican fast-food restaurant.

13-8   Capitalize organizational names when they refer to specific departments or groups within the originator's own organization. Do not use capitals when referring to a department or group in another organization.

I think Marcia works in the Marketing Department.

The Executive Board of our company is in the process of developing a new corporate strategy.

Does he work in their advertising department?

13-9   Capitalize specific brand names but not the product types.

Dove   soap
Mercury   automobile
Hershey   candy
Jantzen   swimsuits
Adler   typewriter

13-5—13-7

a. **B**usiness **L**eaders
b. **R**iver
c. **L**ibrary
d. C
e. C

Proofread the following sentences for capitalization errors. If a sentence is correct, write a *C* to the right of it.

a. Do you use a Ko-Rec-Type Ribbon for your printer?

b. Our human resources Department offers some special benefits.

c. Eileen traded her Dodge Dart Automobile for a Ford Escort.

d. Doesn't everyone love Big mac hamburgers?

e. Did you know that Sheaffer Fountain Pens are making a comeback?

13-10 Capitalize both parts of a hyphenated word *if* they are proper nouns or proper adjectives. Do not capitalize prefixes to proper nouns.

ex-Governor Adams   Mayor-elect Cox
French-American cuisine   mid-Atlantic
North-South game   Spanish-speaking students
New York-Los Angeles flight

Proofread the following sentences for capitalization errors. If a sentence is correct, write a *C* to the right of it.

a. Does the library contain any books on Latin-American culture?

b. Many people suffer from the post-Christmas blues.

c. The Chinese people greeted Ex-president Nixon warmly.

d. In Mid-August the school will open for its seventy-eighth year.

e. In the days of pre-World War II, the nation had a depressed economy.

13-11 Capitalize points of the compass when they refer to definite regions of the country or are used with other proper names. Do not capitalize these words when they indicate a direction.

Rae lives east of the college.

The Pelhams moved to the West Coast.

ABC Moving is located on North Fifth Street.

13-8—13-9

a. ribbon
b. **H**uman **R**esources
c. automobile
d. **M**ac
e. fountain **p**ens

13-10

a. C
b. C
c. **ex-P**resident
d. **m**id-August
e. C

Proofread the following sentences for capitalization errors. If a sentence is correct, write a *C* to the right of it.

a. Plans are to develop the medical complex West of the city.

b. John moved to an apartment on Chicago's North Shore.

c. The south is noted for its gracious hospitality.

d. To see large fields of tulips, drive east for eight miles.

e. Babbler & Sons has been purchased by Western Pacific Company.

13-12   Do not capitalize seasons of the year unless they are portrayed as persons.

summer winds   fall conference   Old Man Winter

 Proofread the following sentences for capitalization errors. If a sentence is correct, write a *C* to the right of it.

a. Farmers' crops are in desperate need of spring rains.

b. To see New England in the Fall of the year is one of my dreams.

c. The poem reads, "And Summer with a nest of robins in her hair . . ."

d. No one has been able to predict the whims of mother nature this year.

e. Would you like to travel to Switzerland next winter for some skiing?

Additional Capitalization Rules

The following guidelines are presented to help you apply capitalization rules correctly in special situations. Rules for nouns followed by numbers, personal titles, and academic degrees are discussed.

13-13   Capitalize most nouns followed by numbers. The words *sentence, page, paragraph, line,* and *verse* should not be capitalized.

13-11
a. **west**
b. C
c. **South**
d. C
e. C

13-12
a. C
b. **fall**
c. C
d. **Mother Nature**
e. C

Chapter 5	page 6
Route 95	paragraph 2
Flight 1034	sentence 1

 Proofread the following sentences for capitalization errors. If a sentence is correct, write a *C* to the right of it.

a. Did the secretary select Model No. 2166 or 2266?

b. The information found in table 3, page 10, should be very helpful.

c. While walking along highway 258, Eddie was stung by a bee.

d. Reserved seats for the concert are located in Section 5.

e. Martha has plans to leave for Ireland on Delta Airlines flight 471.

13-14

Capitalize a title that precedes a person's name.

The meeting was called to order by Chairman Richard Andruzzi.

■ Capitalize a title in an address or signature line.

> Mrs. Leslyn Winn, Vice President
> Willis Chambers, Manager

■ Do not capitalize titles when they *follow* a name in the sentence or are used in place of a name.

James Swanson, editor, received the Outstanding Journalist's Award.

The chairman of the group, Richard Andruzzi, called the meeting to order.

Note: If the official is referred to in formal minutes, rules, or bylaws, an exception is made and the title is always capitalized.

■ Capitalize an official title that refers to a specific person and is a title of high distinction.

the President of the United States	the Prime Minister
the Governor of Arizona	the Secretary of State

13-13

a. C
b. Table
c. Highway
d. C
e. Flight 471

Proofread the following sentences for capitalization errors. If a sentence is correct, write a *C* to the right of it.

a. Calvin Adams, professor of communication, spoke to the American Journalism Association.

b. The Kiwanis Club asked mayor White to be its after-dinner speaker.

c. The U.S. secretary of defense is having budgetary problems.

d. Is it true that the Prime Minister of Canada won the tennis match?

e. The governor of Nebraska will be speaking at commencement.

13-15 Capitalize the name of an academic degree immediately following a personal name whether it is abbreviated or written in full.

> Carol Brooks, M.D.
> Muriel Bloom, Doctor of Philosophy

■ Capitalize the abbreviation of an academic degree.

> B.S.   Ph.D.

■ Do not capitalize an academic degree when used in general terms or with the word *degree*.

> Margo just received her master's.
>
> Does a bachelor of arts degree guarantee a good job?

13-16 Capitalize names of specific course titles but not areas of study (except for proper nouns or adjectives).

> Keyboarding 1   typewriting
> Information Processing 201 American history

13-14

a. C
b. **Mayor**
c. **Secretary** of **Defense**
d. C
e. **Governor**

Proofread the following sentences for capitalization errors. If a sentence is correct, write a *C* to the right of it.

a. Phil has earned his B.S. Degree in chemistry.

b. I will be taking accounting, business law, programming, and English 201 this quarter.

c. The university awarded more than two thousand Bachelor's degrees at its commencement exercises.

d. Many companies require all managerial personnel to have b.a. degrees.

e. Inglis F. Duckett, Doctor of Education, is the author of many books.

Spelling Review

To improve your ability to detect spelling errors, master the words below. Watch for them in this and the final chapter.

acknowledgment	fascinate
apologize	gratitude
embarrass	insistent
emphasize	miniature
equipped	perseverance

Proofreading Tips

Study these tips and apply them as you proofread:

1. Unless you can apply a definite principle that calls for capitalization, do not capitalize.

2. Do not confuse proper nouns with the general uses of the same word.

3. If your workplace has special rules for the use of capitals, follow its style guide.

13-15—13-16

a. **degree**
b. C
c. **bachelor's**
d. **B.A.**
e. C

PROOFREADING APPLICATIONS

Proofread the following paragraphs and use the appropriate proofreading symbols to mark errors you find in capitalization, grammar, and spelling. To aid you in proofreading, the number of errors to be found is indicated in parentheses at the end of Exercises P-1, P-2, and P-3. You must find them on your own in Exercise P-4.

P-1 Last week I gave Mr. Swann, the supply manager, a requisition for the following items: 10 reams bond paper, 6 boxes matching envelopes, 12 Burroughs Ribbons, 1 box Swingline staples, a Dictionary, and 1 box rubber bands. Now Customer Services will be equiped to operate for the next few months. Although I am embarassed to admit it, my request was denied because the Customer Services Department has spent its budget for the year. When Mrs. Alford, our Supervisor, heard this news, she said, "What can we do?" I had only one suggestion: close the office and go home! (6)

P-2 Julie, my secretary, passed the CPS exam the first time she took it! With perseverence, she reviewed publications such as *The Secretary* and *Procedures For The Electronic Office*, obtained study materials from Professional Secretaries International, and attended review courses at Northwestern Community College. An acknowledgment of her success will take place on Monday, October 23, at chester's inn on Unstead Avenue when her CPS pin and certificate will be presented in gratitute by her former employer, Ex-Governor Hunt. (5)

P-3 Everybody at our house is in college except me. Lori is studying Medicine at Wake University. David is attending school on the West Coast but has not declared a major yet. After completing her Master's degree, Lynn has enrolled at Indiana University to pursue a doctor of music degree. Mom is taking an Accounting class at Central Community College, and Dad is learning German. And as for me, I'm a senior at Brewster High School expecting to earn my diploma in the Spring. (4)

P-1

1. ribbons
2. dictionary
3. equipped
4. embarrassed
5. supervisor
6. Close

P-2

1. perseverance
2. *Procedures* for *the Electronic*
3. Chester's Inn
4. gratitude
5. ex-Governor

P-4 Senator Ruth Wallace was to be the speaker at a republican fund raiser. I was responsible for meeting her at the airport. When American Flight 390 arrived, she was not on it. Checking at the American desk, I found that her name was not on the passenger list. Frustrated, I hailed a cab to the Velvet Cloak hotel. Imagine my surprise when I saw the senator heading for the same cab as I! She had arrived on <u>Eastern</u> Flight 390. When I attempted to apolagize, she was insistant that the error was not mine but was made in her office.

P-3

1. medicine
2. master's degree
3. accounting
4. spring

P-4

1. **R**epublican
2. **H**otel
3. **S**enator heading
4. apo**l**ogize
5. insist**e**nt

PROGRESSIVE PROOFREADING

The following section provides an opportunity for you to apply your proofreading skills to a job situation.

You are employed as an assistant to Dr. M. Ellen Schwartz, executive director of the American Business Education Association (ABEA). She is busy planning for the ABEA convention. Your job is to proofread some of the registration materials. Dr. Schwartz uses the block letter style with mixed punctuation.

Job 1: News release.

Job 2: Information sheet about Miami.

Job 3: A letter to be sent to ABEA members prepared from hand-written notes.

AMERICAN BUSINESS EDUCATION ASSOCIATION
1111 South Wabash Street
Chicago, IL 60605-2912

Release Date: February 28, 19--

Over two-thousand A.B.E.A. members are expected to converge on Miami, Florida, when the American business education association thirty-eighth annual convention convenes on March 13. This information comes from Doctor Sue D. Briley, President of the A.E.B.A. Dr. Briley, a Business Education instructor at Parks College, is serving the first year of a two-year term as President.

Using the theme "Get In Touch With The Future," Dr. Briley and her convention committee have planned a program featuring numberous leaders in the business education areas of Accounting, Computer Science, Keyboarding, and Economics.

Approximately 125 textbook publishers and equiptment salespeople are expected to exhibit their products.

The entertainment committee has succeeded in getting well-known Motivational Speaker Zig Ziglar for the luncheon presentation. Internationally famous entertainer Danny Kaye will provide entertainment at the closing banquet. The committee has also planned a jamboree for the fifteenth of March at the Orange Bowl.

The convention will end with a business session on the seventeenth of March.

Dr. M. Ellen Schwartz

Job 2 Proofread the information sheet below, checking for all kinds of errors.

WHERE TO GO AND WHAT TO SEE IN MIAMI IN MARCH

Miami has some especially fasinating activities scheduled for
Mid-March, when ABEA members will be in town. Selected events
listed in this week in Miami, a weekly magazine published by the
Miami chamber of commerce are as follows

1. The Annual Shakespeare festival (March 5-23). Three of the
    great bard's plays are being presented: Two gentleman of
    Verona, Romeo and Julied, and the Tempest.

2. The Dade County Counsel of arts folk festival (March 15-16)
    Featured will be local artists and craftspeople. Admission
    is free.

4. Violinist Itzhak Perlman Concert (March 17). To reserve tickets,
    calll (305) 555-3491.

In addition to these special attractions, the following year-round
activities are available:

   Vizcaya. It is a great italian villa located on Biscayne bay.
   Built by by James Deering in 1912. Admission is $5 for adults
   and $3.50 for children under 12.

   Shoping centers. Two fine ones are mayfair mall, a high-fashion
   boutique center, and miracle mile, a four-block shopping
   extravaganza in Coral Gables.

   Bus tours and harbor cruises. Check at your hotel desk for
   details.

To travel outside the city, you might consider renting a Century
or Thrifty car and traveling North to fort Lauderday or South to
Key West. You can take highway 1 to each of these cities.

Job 3 Proofread the letter on page 193 by comparing it to the handwritten notes below. Dr. Schwartz uses the block letter style with mixed punctuation.

Notes about ABEA meeting:

38th convention

Miami, Fla., at Palms Hotel (get address)

March 13 to 17

theme: get in touch with the future

— seminar topic example, "Experiential Learning --The Educational Tool for the Future"

— reservations should be sent directly to the hotel at 2552 3d Ave., SW, 33129-0615; can guarantee reservation on Amex card by Feb. 28 if members want to stay at the convention hotel.

— registration form (in December issue of ABEA Journal); check should be returned to this office by Feb. 15

AMERICAN BUSINESS EDUCATION ASSOCIATION
1111 South Wabash Street
Chicago, IL 60605-2912

January 13, 19--

Dr. Peggy Martin, professor
School of Business Education
Eastern University
1072 East 5th Street
Charleston, Ill.

Dear Mrs. Martin:

Make your plans now to head South in late Winter to attend the American Business Education assoc iation's annual convention. The Palms hotel in Miami, FL, will be the sight for this 38th meeting, which begins on March 13 and ends on March 17.

"Get In Touch With The Future" is the theme of this year's convention. Several new, pertinent topics have been added, one of which is "Experimental Learning--The Educational Tool for the Future."

Send your hotel registration directly to the Palms Hotel, 2525 Third Avenue, S.W., Miami, FL 33129-0615, no later than February 28 to ensure a room at the convention hotel. You may guarantee your reservation by including your Am. express card number.

To register for the convention, complete the registration form that is in the December issue of the ABEA journal. Mail it along along with your check to this office by Feb. 15.

Plan to attend the opening session followed by the Orange Bowl Jamboree; a watch containing a minature TV will be given away as a door prize.

Please extend an invitation to students, and emphasise the value of participating in a conference designed for professional growth.

Very Truly Yours

M. Ellen Schwarts

AA

Chapter 14

Proofreading for Content Errors

Objectives: *After completing this chapter, you should be able to*

1. Identify errors caused by incorrect facts, inconsistencies, and missing information.
2. Recognize errors resulting from language stereotyping, redundancy, and word choice.
3. Use appropriate proofreading symbols to indicate changes in text.

Proofreading for Effective Communication

The real measure of a proofreader's skill lies in the ability to proofread written communication for meaning and accuracy and to edit and revise ineffective communication. While previous chapters have dealt primarily with mechanical or grammatical errors, this chapter addresses the need to proofread for content errors—errors that affect the clarity, correctness, and meaning of the message.

A good proofreader realizes that the clarity of the message depends upon copy that has no incorrect facts, no inconsistencies, no missing information, no language stereotyping, no redundancies, no inaccurate word choices, and no grammatical errors. The skillful proofreader must be able to identify these problems, make necessary changes, or bring questionable items to the originator's attention. You have already learned the appropriate symbols for making corrections to copy. If the correction is not obvious, use the following proofreading symbol to query the originator.

　　(?)　　Query the originator.

```
The new employee's social security number
is 273-62-901.
```

Incorrect Facts

When copy contains incorrect facts, confusion and frustration can result. It is not always easy to recognize such errors unless there is a rough draft or source document that can be used for comparison. However, there are items within the document that the proofreader should always check for accuracy. If the copy makes reference to

Wednesday, June 16, and June 16 is actually on Thursday, there is an obvious error. If figures are used, an error can sometimes be recognized by using reason and common sense. Zip codes, unusual or unfamiliar names, invoice numbers, telephone numbers, social security numbers, and other items of special importance should always be checked.

14-1   Eliminate incorrect facts in copy by correcting any inaccuracies in dates, figures, addresses, names, and numbers or by querying the originator. Note the incorrect facts in the examples below.

The Dow Jones Industrial Average rose from 1910 to 1942, a gain of 22 points.

The play is scheduled for February 15-30. _15-28 ?_

 Proofread the following sentences for incorrect facts.

a. The convention will be held from Monday, August 11, through Friday, August 18.

b. The telephone number of the new bookstore is (817) 555-210.

c. Purchasing the unit at 15 percent off the regular price of $400 will allow me to save $80.

d. This year's meeting will be held in the "Mile-High City" of Denver, Connecticut, on May 29.

e. The consultant's address is P.O. Box 412, Anchorage, AL 99506-6133.

Inconsistencies

Whenever reference is made to specific information more than once in a document, be sure that the information appears consistently. For example, if a person's name appears more than once in a letter, check the spelling for consistency. If there are two acceptable spellings for a word, the same spelling should be used throughout. If numbers are transferred from one document to another, be sure the numbers have been copied correctly. If a block style is chosen for a letter, make certain that the style is used consistently in the letter.

14-2 Eliminate inconsistencies in copy by checking words, figures, and format for any discrepancies. Note the inconsistencies in the following examples.

Mr. Dakas was elected mayor in 1986; Dacas has been an exemplary public official.

This tape player can be purchased for only $189—where else can you find a unit like this for $199?

Proofread the following sentences for inconsistencies.

a. Henry Schmidt founded Schmidtt Associates on July 10, 1910.

b. The AAIS (Association of American Information Systems) is hosting its tenth annual convention; the registration fee for AIAS members is $45.

c. According to Miss Amhurst—and I agree with Mrs. Amhurst—the results of the program will not be immediately obvious.

d. We questioned why so few have really benefited when all should have benefitted.

e. Three of our 28 games have been victories, although the end of this 29-game season is three months away.

Missing Information

In addition to the types of errors already discussed, other factors can affect the meaning of the message. For example, words, phrases, or even complete lines or sentences are sometimes omitted unintentionally. Therefore, it is necessary to compare the final copy with the rough-draft copy to be sure nothing has been deleted. If the proofreader is not authorized to edit and make changes, errors that prevent the meaning from being clear must be called to the attention of the originator.

14-3 Eliminate confusion in copy by checking for missing information. Notice how missing information in the following examples makes the meaning unclear.

To get to the airport, turn right on this road.

14-1

a. Monday, August 11 ?

Friday, August 18 ?

b. 555-210 ?

c. $80 ?

d. Denver, Connecticut   Colorado

e. AL   K

14-2

a. Schmidt Schmidtt
b. AAIS
c. Miss Amhurst
   Mrs. Amhurst
d. benefited benefitted
e. 28 games 29-game-season

Proofread the following sentences for missing information.

a. The car you ordered will be shipped Monday, October.

b. Make a turn at the intersection of Patterson Road and Spartan Drive to reach my office.

c. Please deliver a 3 x 5 frame on Monday.

d. To stop the screen from automatically rolling, press a button.

e. To stop your car from skidding on ice, turn your wheel in that direction.

Language Stereotyping

Today's society frowns upon the stereotyping of particular jobs or roles as either "men's work" or "women's work" because men and women are now employed in a greater number of occupations than they once were. Using the pronouns *she* or *he* alone to refer to a person may be incorrect and reflect stereotyping.

14-4 Eliminate *he* or *she* from copy when it is impossible to determine which pronoun is accurate.

> *not* Who is the lawyer and what is his address?

> *but* What is the name and address of the lawyer?

■ Use a plural noun and *their* to avoid using gender-specific pronouns.

> *not* A good teacher praises his students.

> *but* Good teachers praise their students.

■ Address the reader in the second person to avoid using gender-specific pronouns.

> Praise your students.

■ Reword the sentence to avoid the use of gender-specific pronouns.

> *not* Each contestant signed *her* entry form.

> *but* Each contestant signed *an* entry form.

14-3

a. October?
b. a ? turn
c. 3 × 5
d. a ? button
e. that direction

■ Use neutral terms when referring to both men and women.

businessperson, business people	*not* businessman
salesperson, sales representative	*not* salesman
mail carrier	*not* mailman
members of Congress, representatives	*not* congressmen
people, humanity	*not* mankind
flight attendant	*not* stewardess

 Proofread the following paragraph for language stereotyping and make any necessary corrections.

Every person likes to be appreciated for the work he does. For example, a secretary who does good work desires acknowledgment by her employer; a salesman with an excellent sales record enjoys praise from his manager; a nurse whose skills are outstanding desires recognition by her supervisor; and a stewardess whose capabilities are above average likes praise from her superior. The supervisor who takes time to compliment his employees is certain to benefit as well from the increased morale that positive reinforcement can create.

Redundancy and Wordiness

Repetition is often used to reinforce ideas. However, when a word or phrase unnecessarily repeats an idea, the real point of the communication can become camouflaged, creating confusion for the reader. Using several words when one will serve is termed *redundancy*. Wordy terms can be written concisely or deleted as illustrated in the following frame.

14-5 Rewrite redundant expressions to eliminate unnecessary words.

Redundant Expressions	Alternatives
at the present time	now
completely eliminated	eliminated
despite the fact that	although
end result	result
exact same	same
important, essential points	essentials
in the event that	should

14-4

a. People like . . . **they** do
b. secretaries who do good work desire . . . **their** employers
c. sales **staff**
d. from **their** managers
e. nurses . . . desire . . . by **their** supervisors
f. **flight attendants** . . . like
g. **their** superiors
h. Supervisors . . . take . . . **their** employees are

past experience	experience
personal opinion	opinion
whether or not	whether

■ Delete entire expressions that are unnecessary.

to take this opportunity
permit me to say
for the purpose of
I wish to

 Proofread the following paragraph for redundancies and make any necessary corrections.

Two events are planned for our company's spring picnic. First and foremost, there will be a softball game. Second, after the ball game, there will be a barbecue. From past experience I know that these events combined together should provide us with an evening of fun. Whether or not we have fun, though, will be up to each and every one of us.

Word Choice

A common problem in written communications is the use of words or phrases that are so overworked that they are no longer effective. Such expressions are termed *clichés*; they reflect an unoriginal writer and produce a bored reader. When proofreading, be alert for clichés. Make tactful suggestions to the originator to eliminate clichés and to insert more effective words.

14-6 Proofread to eliminate clichés.

Clichés	Alternatives
a word to the wise	a caution
after all is said and done	when
as plain as day	obvious
by leaps and bounds	rapidly
contact me	telephone, inform
few and far between	scarce
in this day and age	today
last but not least	last
nipped in the bud	stopped
stick to your guns	persevere
the almighty dollar	money

14-5
a. First, there
b. From experience,
c. combined should
d. whether we
e. each of us

Proofread the following paragraph for clichés and make any necessary corrections

The sales staff will meet at the crack of dawn (7:30 a.m.) on Thursday in the Red Room. The agenda will focus on the recent growth of sales. We hope to give this sales record an in-depth examination, not just a tip-of-the iceberg glance. After all is said and done, it may be as plain as day that the almighty dollar alone motivated these sales. Last but not least, we will also discuss a new employee benefit account. A word to the wise—don't miss this important meeting!

Spelling Review

14-6

To improve your ability to detect spelling errors, master the words below. Watch for them in the end-of-chapter activities.

analyst	independent
efficiency	insurance
exaggerate	merchandise
fluctuating	productivity
implemented	programmer

a. at 7:30 a.m.
b. not just a glance
c. a glance. It
d. may be obvious
e. that money
f. sales. We
g. account. Don't

Proofreading Tips

Study these tips and apply them as you proofread:

1. The proofreader must read the copy with a questioning mind. Is the message perfectly clear? Are there any inconsistencies in the presentation of facts? Do obsolete expressions or language stereotyping detract from the meaning of the message? Are there omissions or redundancies?

2. Control the environment in which you proofread—noise and movement are distractions. Be sure there is sufficient light.

3. Verify the spelling of names.

4. When revising copy, cross out all unnecessary original copy.

PROOFREADING APPLICATIONS

Proofread the following exercises and use the appropriate proof-reading symbols to mark errors you find in content, grammar, and spelling. To aid you in proofreading, the number of errors to be found is indicated in parentheses at the end of Exercises P-1, P-2, and P-3. You must find them on your own in Exercise P-4.

P-1 Approaching the intersection, the policeman saw the collision between the two cars. While the officer directed traffic around the accident, the victims were helped from their cars by a television newsman and a photographer, who were filming a news story nearby. The drivers, a female lawyer and a stewardess, were slightly injured. They were taken to the medical center where their injuries were treated by a male nurse. (5)

P-2 You are invited to attend a three-hour unadvertised sale exclusively for charge customers on Tuesday, May 10. The doors will open at 6 p.m. and will remain open until 10 p.m. All spring merchandize will be reduced from 20 to 40 percent. A selection of our linen suits, formerly priced at $240, will be reduced 30 percent. That means a saving to you of $82. The sale will be open to the public on Thursday, May 13. For the best selection of our sale merchandise, plan to join us on Tuesday evening, May 11. (5)

P-3 Branch Bank and Trust Company is opening its new office complex on Thursday, August 7. A pair of two exciting events is scheduled for that date. First and foremost is the ribbon-cutting ceremony at 10 a.m. Mayor Mark Johnson, he will do the honors. President Alan Gumbel will then give the dedicatory address. Immediately following the address is the second exciting event of the day—the center will hold an open house.

The bank is proud of this new center due to the fact that it is the first one to be built in this region. At this point in time, only the first three floors are occupied. However, the consensus of opinion is that full occupancy is expected by then. (7)

P-1

1. police **officer** saw
2. television
   news**reporter**
3. a lawyer
4. and a **flight attendant**
5. treated by a **nurse**

P-2

1. attend a **four**-hour
2. merchandise
3. a saving to you of **$72**
4. Thursday, May **12**
5. Tuesday evening,
   May **10**

P-4 This ad appeared in the Sunday *Phoenix Sun*. Miss Willson is ordering one of the pins. Proofread her letter.

```
                    November 5, 19--


                    Kohl's Jewelers
                    P.O. Box 1353
                    Phoenix, AR  85334-1353

                    Ladies and Gentlemen

                    Please send me one initial pin as shown in your ad in Sun-
                    day's Phoenix Sun.  I want it in silver with the initials
                    LMB.  Please send it to me at the above address.  A check
                    for $19.95 is enclosed.

                    Very truly yours


                    Anne E. Willson
```

PROGRESSIVE PROOFREADING

The following section provides an opportunity for you to apply your proofreading skills to a job situation:

You are manager of TOPS (Temporary Office Personnel Services) in New Orleans, Louisiana. This business is one of three branches of a new business venture owned by Mary Dunstan, who resides in Baton Rouge, Louisiana. Your office provides two services to local business firms: It provides temporary office help to them, and it also contracts to provide certain office jobs to be done in-house. At the present time, you are to proofread all work that has been done. The agency uses the block letter style with open punctuation. Today you have the following items:

Job 1: A letter to the owner of TOPS.

Job 2: An article entitled "Is Flexplace in Your Vocabulary?" that is being prepared for publication.

Job 3: An article entitled "Stretch Your Travel Dollar" that will become a part of a brochure published by the local travel agency.

P-3

1. a pair of exciting
2. First is
3. Mark Johnson will
4. new center **because**
5. **Now** only the
6. consensus is
7. is expected (specific date)

P-4

1. No return address
2. AR should be AZ
3. $19.95 should be $22.90
4. No enclosure

Job 1 Proofread the following letter for content and mechanical errors.

TOPS
(Temporary Office Personnel Services)
909 Linden Avenue
New Orleans, LA 70128-9400

August 15, 19--

Ms. Mary Dunstan
2001 King Alfred Drive
Baton Rogue, LO 71304-6421

Dear Ms. Dunstan

Since you asked me to make suggestions for improving the efficiency
of TOPS, I am writing to share with you an idea that I believe
will have a very postive effect on the productivity of this office.
I am eager to hear your reaction.

Recently I had the opportunity to examine a new publication from
South-Western Publishing Company entitled Programmed Proofreading.
I believe we should ask each temporary office employee to work
through this publication before beginning an actual assignment with
us. The payoff in productivity and accuracy will, in my opinion
be well worth the cost of the books.

At the present time, I am spending quite a bit of time proofreading
the documents produced by our employees. Many of the errors that
I rather frequently find are addressed in the book. Working through
exercises that contain those errors will impress upon our employees
the importance of absolute accuracy. While I would continue to
proofread the documents. I believe my proofreading time would
be cut considerably.

There are thirteen chapters in the Programmed Proofreading book.
I found Chapter 12 on content errors to be especially helpful.

Sincerely

Charles Daniels

JP

IS FLEXPLACE IN YOUR VOCABULARY?

Some years ago, many organizations adopted "flextime," making it possible, beyond a shadow of a doubt, for employees to juggle work schedules and home responsibilites. At this point in time, there is <u>flexplace</u> (sometimes referred to as "telecommute").

<u>What Is "Flexplace"</u>?

The flexplace arrangement enables employees to do all or part of their work away from the corporate office. Various forms of decentralized workplaces are possible; satellite offices, or branch offices that are linked electronically to main offices, neighborhood offices that are shared by employees of different companies, and employee's homes.

<u>For Whom is It Designed</u>?

Flexplace is best implemented in information-intensive firms that have computers, networks, and data bases installed: banks, insurance companies, and financial institutions. Managers and professionals who work independently, as well as computer specialists and women who are secretaries and data entry specialists, are best suited for flexplace. Consider these cases:

Disabled from a severe accident, Leslie Longhill works at home as a program analyst, her computer is linked by phone lines to clients' computers and to her companies computer. Allan and Lorraine Templeton operate a consulting business for a large cor-poration. Loraine also works part-time as a programmer for a large corporation. A typesetting firm employs Janet Gabor to meet its fluctuating needs. Jane, mother of three young children,

burns the candle at both ends because she is also fullfilling

family responsibilities.
<u>Advantages of Flexplace</u>

Some employers consider flexplace as a way to reduce costs,

to attract personal whom would not otherwise be available for

employment, and increasing productivity. A large insurance comp-

any estimated that 16 home-based persons produced 50 percent more

than persons working at the office. Another computer company re-

ported a 35 per cent increase in productivity.

In this day and age when people are seeking an alternative

to the high costs and frustrations of commuting to work, many

persons consider that the freedom of workplace may be an important

benefit. Flextime enables persons who are self-motivated, on the

ball, and who manage their time well to work independantly. How-

ever, caution must be exercised that working at home doesn't

become all work and no play. Working at home can create additional

stress by making it impossible to escape the demands of the office.

<u>Conclusion</u>

Is flexplace for you? Despite the fact that it may not be

feasible or possible for all workers, it may be apporpriate for

others. Research and experimentation by organizations that are

willing to establish "telework" arrangements will reveal whether

or not flexible working arrangements are viable.

Job 3   Proofread the following article; be alert for misspellings.

STRETCH YOUR TRAVEL DOLLAR

The cost of obtaining money to travel abroad is often over-
looked in travel budgets. Here are some important essential
tips for those planning to travel abroad soon:

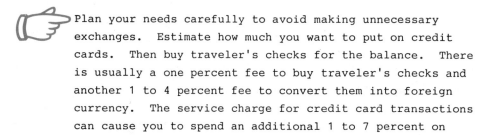Plan your needs carefully to avoid making unnecessary
exchanges. Estimate how much you want to put on credit
cards. Then buy traveler's checks for the balance. There
is usually a one percent fee to buy traveler's checks and
another 1 to 4 percent fee to convert them into foreign
currency. The service charge for credit card transactions
can cause you to spend an additional 1 to 7 percent on
money exchange.

Look for the best deal on traveler's checks. You usually
pay twice when you use traveler's checks--when you buy
them and when you convert them. Try to find an outlet
that does not impose a sales charge.

Consider the value of the dollar. In the event that the
dollar declines, it will buy less. If you think the value
of the dollar will decrease before you take your trip,
consider prepaid tour packages so that costs will remain
stable. Traveler's checks issued in foriegn currency
provide another safeguard against a weekening dollar.

Consider using European Currency Units. ECUs consit of
10 common market currencies and are accepted in countries
where traveler's checks are accepted. They are sold at
some european banks and at european offices of Am. Express.

Choose credit cards wisely. A travel agent can advice
you, but you must decide whether his advice meets your
needs. Travel and entertainment cards offer the best

services for travelers who run short of cach, but the
annual fees are higher. Some Credit Cards offer revolving
credit and have lower service fees but interest is charged
if cash advances are made. A recent survey of issuing
banks showed a range in interest rates from 12.5% to 21%--
a difference of 7.5 percent. It at all times pays to shop
around.

Compare exchange costs. The best choices for exchange
are large banks, they usually offer better rates than
airports and railroad stations. You will usually find
a good exchange rate from the company that issued your
traveler's checks.

Protect your cash and your credit cards. Exchangeing several
small traveler's checks is expensive and costly, but that
cost must be weighed against the disadvantage of carrying
more cash. You may be interested in investing in a wallet
made especially for traveling. Some hang around the neck;
others go around the waist. Safeguard your credit cards
by making photocopies of it before you leave.

Spend your coins wisely. Although easier said than done,
use your foreign coins before you leave each country, since
they can't be converted. Finally, keep enough American
dollars to get you home safely.

Posttest

Proofread each of the following sentences, and use proofreading symbols to indicate changes that should be made. If a sentence is correct, write "C" after it. Solutions to the Posttest begin on page 231.

1. Each report will require six sheets of 8½- by 11-inch paper.

2. After welcoming faculty and students, the revised schedule was distibuted.

3. As you travel north on interstate 55 to Los Angels, turn off at the Vine Ave. exit.

4. An embarrasing article about the company in a computre trade publication.

5. Lynn and Dawn was in band practice at South high school for three hours.

6. Keyboardin and listening skills continues to be prerequites for office employees

7. The criteria for entering the contest has been changed.

8. Neither Jerry nor Bob have the diskettes he needs for the FORTRAN class.

9. Here is the insturctions: Every desk and chair has to be removed from the offices.

10. Everybody was pleased that the number of late registrants were smaller than before.

11. If Doctor Chas. Wrenn, an officer in the A.M.A., takes flight 128 at 12 noon E.S.T., he will arrive in Portland at 1 p.m. PST.

12. Jade objects found in China included pendants,bracelets and hairpins.

13. All salespeople on the team did their jobs well.

14. The team voted to hold their practice session on Friday night.

15. Have you and her decided whether to take Spanish or Accounting next fall?

16. Chris is the one whom will receive the award.

17. Keith had neither completed the payroll nor making a deposit, but the company mailed it's monthly report on Wenesday anyway.

18. Mr. C. R. Lewis, business manager, is working on his m.b.a. at Tulane University.

19. It will take us about twenty-five years to repay the principal on our home mortgage.

20. The capital of New Mexico, Santa Fe, is located in the north-central part of the state.

21. The waiter brought French dressing, but I had ordered Italian dressing.

22. You should notify our Personnel Department prior to a planed absence.

23. Mark won a Zenith color television.

24. The UPI reported that Ex-President Ford is planning a campaign tour of the Southwest

25. Information about the winter conference is on page 18 of section 3 of today's paper.

26. The article was sent by federal express on Nov. 10 and it reached the governor on the 11th.

27. The committee sent a terse reminder to the 8 people, who were delinquent.

28. Look! That house is on fire.

29. About 500 more studnets are enrolled in the class—an increase of eight percent.

30. I would prefer someone, who has had experience with an envirnmental agency.

31. The article "Should I By Gold and Silver Now?" contains some very good references, including the book "Investing in Metals and Coins."

32. Gloria's telephone number appeared as 555-455.

33. All of the subscription money had been turned in and Chairman Volpe offered congradulations for a job well done.

34. Jane Maier said, " I proofread the letter and did not find an error.

35. On January 10, 1988, Stewart Mays, President of Baldwin College, will present a lecture entitled The Benefits of Desktop Publishing."

36. Your deposit will be refunded by the fifteenth of April, of course; but you must make your request be March 31st.

37. I am sending the material by certified mail, return reciept requested.

38. Announcments of the meeting were sent to the following people: Timothy Cloud, director of production Annette Pilgreen, director of marketing, and Susan Stansbury, director of sales.

39. The advise "Get hooked on Seafood" seems to bee scientifically sound.

40. It was a long hot humid summer; therefore, we spent alot of time at the beach.

41. The doors open at 9 o'clock, so I'll meet you for coffee at 10.

42. When you receive the letter, sign your name on the enclosed form, attach your check for $15.50 and send the form and check to me.

43. Dial 555-811 and give (1) your name, (2) your address, (3 your telephone number and (4) your date of birth.

44. Begin your exercize plan by swimming a moderate number of laps (15 and then rest.

45. A copy of the original Declaration of Independence—the 22d to be located—was found in North Carolina in 1983 and sold at an auction for $135,000.00.

46. In slow measured tones, General Harnett read the famous document to a gatherin of 3,250 people.

47. A panda cub which weighed 3½ ounces at berth, was born to a bear weighing 237 pounds.

48. Will you refer to Chapter 15, Page 13, for the story of the farmers's plight.

49. Did you know that in 1986 20 of 150 people failed the law examination?

50. If the first line of a letter address is "Ms. Louise Forehand," the salutation should be "Dear Ms. Forhand," not "Dear Madam".

Solutions

Pretest Solution

Pretest

Proofread the following sentences for errors and write in your suggested changes. Indicate a correct sentence by writing "C" after it. Each sentence is worth two points. Solutions to the Pretest are on page 213.

1. A number of responses has been received from the February 5th mailing.
2. Tom and Julie have gone to the store on Warren road to get five gals. of paint.
3. Bacon and eggs is a traditional breakfast dish in the South. C
4. Ansering the telephone and filing is considered routine office tasks. C
5. The secretary, as well as the manager, is attending the time-management workshop. C
6. Each Kaypro computer and Juki printer have a won-year garantee.
7. Neither Enjou nor Tai are enrolled in Business Law 2142, a graduation requirement.
8. Here are the stationary and the No. 10 envelopes that were omitted from your order.
9. The news bulletin reported that Gen. Arnold's plane would arrive at Kennedy International airport at 10:00 a.m.
10. Their personnell committee reviewing applications for the vacancy.
11. While running up the stairs, my shoe fell off.
12. The spelling test included these words: quanity, psychology, similiar, and incidently.
13. An artist conveys more than one thought through his paintings.
14. The board voted it's approval of the preformance of the company's officers.
15. Everyone except Leona Peterson and he attended the conference.
16. That lady to whom the award was given said the idea was her's.
17. He gave the following assignment: You must read Life On The Mississippi.
18. The State of Pennsylvania is also known as the Keystone State.
19. A Mid-August survey revealed that many Americans declared French fries to be their favorite food.
20. Installing a computer in our Records Management Department, will increase its efficiency.
21. The clerk was insistant that those 3 sweaters I bought during the Fall sale could not be returned for any reason.
22. Read chapter five, entitled "Applying for an Executive Assistant's Position," in Wagner's book, *Procedures For The Professional Executive Assistant.*
23. Ms. Dorene Randal, a Yale alumnus, received her m.a. from Duke university and was recomended for a doctoral fellowship by Dr. D. R. Brandon.
24. the governor of Louisianna flew to the Far East to seek industry for his state.
25. I know that a representative will give his personal opinion whether he is asked for it.

26. I would like to hire Debbie Ladd who has all ready had two years' experience.
27. Terry, I found three quarters, one dime and twelve pennies—a total of 92 cents.
28. We use the book "Programmed Proofreading" in our introduction to Transcription course, which meets at 9 o'clock each day.
29. Jim's itinerary for Dec. 31, 1987, was completed by 5 p. m. on September 6th.
30. Nine charter members of this chapter of the AMS (Administrative Managment Society) have failed to mail there renewal checks for $110.00.
31. Andy exclaimed, "Stop! The drawbridge is open!"
32. Over 200 of approximately 3,000 customers are behind in their payments.
33. Rhonda says she understnds the economic principal, but she doesn't think it applies in this case.
34. There will, of course, be a charge for maintainance after the warranty expires.
35. In Chapter 4, Page 14, the following rule appears: Do not divide a word containing 5 or fewer letters.
36. My purchase came to $3.13, and tax was $.13, making a total of $3.62.
37. You will develop the following skills: listening, transcription and proofreading.
38. The old, dilapidated house will be replaced by a lovely two-story house.
39. This is where your twin, Don, lives, is it not? C
40. In Math 465 49% of the class failed the final examination.
41. If your voice tends to drop as you utter the expression, then the expression is nonessential; if your voice tends to rise the expression is essential.
42. The travel agent said, "Your final payment for the November 1 cruise is due on September 1, thirty days prior to departure."
43. The word "telecommuting" has now become a part of the office worker's every day vocabulary and should be a familiar term to all involved in the business world.
44. The sign read "Keep the Place Neat," but children's toys were scattered everywhere.
45. I do plan to take a cruise on the Mississippi River before the cruise company's special expires; however, circumstances prevent me going at this point in time.
46. Twenty-nine of the problems were correct; thats over one half of the total number.
47. Please deliver twelve six-ounce steaks for the party being held at 220 4th Street.
48. Don and Jan's car cost $15,000, and they obtained a loan with 2.9% interest.
49. The letter was signed by Earl Dunn, but the reference initials read "cd:ec." Why? C
50. Of all the books you sent me, there was only one I liked—*The Walk West.* C

Chapter 2

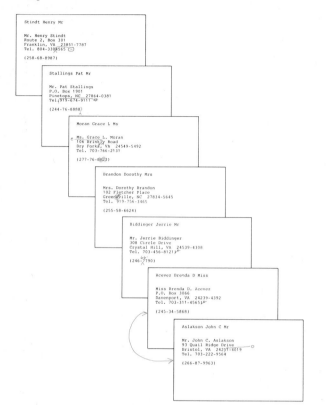

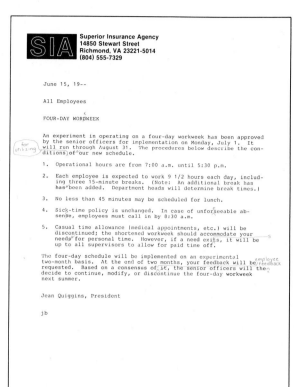

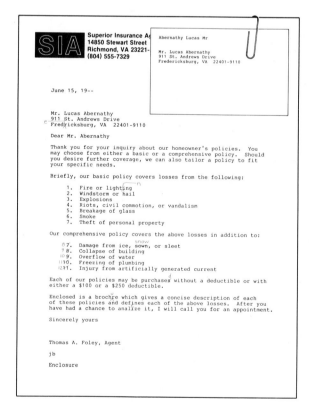

February 15, 19--

(Letter Address)

Dear (Title and Surname)

Congradulations! You are now the proud owner of a STAR
personal computer. We know that you are going to enjoy
using it.

PC Land offers a one-hour training course to each new
customer. It includes instruction on taking care of your
computer, handling diskettes, and copying master disks.

A full line of software, including programs for spread-
sheets, word processing, file management, and games is
available to you at PC Land. Classes with trained
instructors are available with the purchase of any soft-
wear package. Please ask about these classes.

maintenance Although the STAR has definitly proved itself to be
relatively maintainance free, you can secure a service
contract customized to your needs. STAR computers come
ninety with a ninty-day warranty and a one-year guarantee on
the disk drives. Our service center honors warranties
form other STAR dealers as well.

Please call us at 555-2114 or write to us at 125 North
First St. should you desire further information. We are
here to serve you.

Very truly yours

Mr. Tomoko R. Okano
Sales Representative

Customer Names and Addresses

1. Ms. Carmen Alvarez
   4012 Exeter Drive, N.E.
   Rocky Mount, NC 27801-4439

2. Mr. David Tyler
   1518 Bennett Street
   Washington, NC 27889-6902

3. Mrs. Charles Varlashkin
   P.O. Box 30651
   New Bern, NC 28560-5713

4. Mr. D.L. Pate Sr.
   217-B North Meade Street
   Greenville, NC 27834-4209

5. Dr. Jacqueline Harris
   470 Shoreline Drive Avenue
   Elizabeth City, NC 27909-8261

6. Mr. Christopher Churchill
   1036 Dogwood Trail
   Greenville, NC 27835-3479

7. Mr. Kevin Curran
   8941 Graystone Lane
   Pinetops, NC 27864-2297

8. Ms. Susan Haines
   253 Windsor Blvd. Boulevard
   Greenville, NC 27834-6140

9. Mr. Jim Gothard
   602 Fairview Drive
   Wilson, NC 27893-4230

10. Ms. Geo. Herndon
    2018 Garrett Avenue
    Farmville, NC 27828-9817

11. Ms. Valerie Beckman
    301-C Westbrook Apartments
    105 South 11th Street
    Goldsboro, NC 27530-6346

12. Sen. Jackson
    1442 18th Street, SE
    Jacksonville, NC 28540-7294

SPECIAL NOTICE

STAR USERS GROUP

Organizational Meeting

You are invited to attend the initial meeting of
the STAR Computer Users Group to be held in the Prince
Room of the Tryon Hotel on Feb. 20 at 7:30 p.m.

The STAR Users Group will meet monthly to discuss
PC-related topics. Guest speakers from industry will
share how the are using their STARs. New products,
software, and PC-compatible peripherals will be demonstrated and discussed by the manufacturers. These
product demonstrations will be videotaped and made
available to chapter members to hear and see.

Anyone using or interested in STAR computers, software, and STAR-compatible products is eligable to join,
so pass this announcement along to you friends. The
goals of the STAR Users Group are to provide a network
so that all members will be able to use their computers
most effectively and to keep manufacturers aware of the
consumer's needs.

Members attending the first organizational meeting
will determine the best time and location of the monthly
meetings and will appoint a nominating comittee for board
meetings. members

Remember: February 20, 7:30 p.m. Tryon Hotel

Chapter 4

Partners, Inc.
1110 Logan Street
Denver, CO 80203-9176 (303) 555-6478

January 10, 19--

Pat Hamilton, Station Manager

PUBLIC ANNOUNCEMENT

For the past four years, your station has very generously adver-
tised the Partners' Auction as a public service announcement. The
Partners' Auction is held annually to raise money to support proj-
jects for the youth in our community. Can we count on your continued support this year?

If your response is Yes, and we hope it will be, would you please
read the news release that is enclosed over the air begining January
January 29 and running through Febuary 5.

Joseph A. Ramirez, Executive Secretary

re

Enclosure

Partners, Inc.
1110 Logan Street
Denver, CO 80203-9176
(303) 555-6478

NEWS RELEASE

January 10, 19--

For Release January 29, 19--

FIFTH ANNUAL PARTNERS' AUCTION

The Fifth Annual Partners' Auction will be telecast on W.R.-
A.L.-TV from noon to midnight on Saturday, February 5. Lo-
Local merchants have generously donated approximately 1,575 gifts.
You can bid on any of them by calling one of the numbers listed on your television screen. The retail value will be given for
each item, and it will be sold to the highest bidder. All persons working with the auction donate their time; thus all proceeds go directly to Partners to aid the youth of our community.

###

BULLETIN

PARTNERS' AUCTION
Scott Pavilion
Saturday, February 5, 19--

Here is the work schedule for the Partners' Auction. To assure
that each shift is replaced promptly, please arrive at the Pavil-
lion 15 minutes before your assigned starting time.

Time	Volunteers
12 noon to 3 p.m.	David C. Thomas
	Suzanne Trifunovic
	Rhonda Wood
	George Yon
3 p.m. to 5 p.m.	Rodney Dibble
	Sharon Kennedy
	Edward McMillan — Scott Smith
	Winton Woodard
6 p.m. to 9 p.m.	Terry Boiter
	Eileen Deforge
	Joseph Fuller
	Clement Nelson
	June Shavitz
9 p.m. to 12 midnight	Leslie Hagan
	Marie Parrish
	Kimberly Popatak
	Woodrow Windstead Jr
	Janie White

January 15, 19--

(Letter Address)

Ladies and Gentlemen

Mark your calendars for the Fifth Annual Partners' Auction
to be held on Saturday, February 5, in Scott Pavilion.
The auction is sponsored by area businesses for the benefit of Partners, Inc., an organization devoted to helping the youth of the community. As a loyal supporter of
Partners, you know how vital the auction is as a means of
raising funds for the organization.

WRAL-TV will telecast the action from noon to midnight.
As each item is put up for bid, it will be shown on television, and its retail value will be given. You can
place your bid for any item by calling the numbers listed on television. Should your bid be for more than the
retail value, the difference between the two is deductible on your taxes.

Persons working at the auction are volunteering their
services; therefore, all proceeds go directly to Partners.
We hope you will participate in Partners' biggest fund-
raiser of the year. When Partners benefits, the entire
community benefits.

Sincerely yours

Joseph A. Ramirez
Executive Secretary

re

Solutions

Chapter 5

SHOULD YOU USE A REAL ESTATE AGENT?

Do you need a real estate agent when you buy or sell a house? Your immediate response might be that enlisting the help of a professional would be unnecessary. However, unless you have plenty of time and lots of experience, you could be taking a large risk if you do not seek the help of a professional realtor.

An agent can provide buyers with pertinent information to help them meet their location needs. The requirements of a family with a 10-year old child will be different from those of a couple with grown children. The proximity of a good school and recreational facilities is important to parents with young children.

A professional agent can also advise a buyer on an affordable price range based on yearly income. For example, should a buyer with an income of $35,000 be looking at homes in the $90,000 range? An experienced agent would advise the buyer to spend no more than two and one half times gross income. Debt factors, however, must also be considered.

Once the buyer has found a suitable house, the agent can guide the buyer through the transaction by helping to negotiate a price and by putting the buyer in touch with mortgage lenders, contractors, appraisers, inspectors, and insurance agents.

A professional realtor can also save a seller time, money, and frustration. Too often a homeowner seeks the help of a professional only after having incurred problems. One seller spent $350 on advertising, $300 on travel showing the house, $78.25 on phone calls,

---

2

and $800 on maintenance while the house was on the market (a total of $1,528.25). Additionally, the client suffered a great deal of frustration before engaging a professional realtor.

When enlisting the help of a real estate agent, keep the following points in mind:

1. Ask for references from clients who have bought property recently.

2. Investigate the community in which you are interested.

3. Deal with a professional agent "who has a good reputation."

4. Find out if the company which the realtor represents belongs to the local real estate board.

By taking advantage of an agent's experience, access to properties, and information about the local real estate market, people can avoid the pitfalls inherent in purchasing or marketing their homes.

DAR
Delhi Association of Realtors
325 Alabama Street
Indianapolis, IN 46204-6154
(317) 555-7355

MINUTES OF MEETING
DELHI ASSOCIATION OF REALTORS

Place of Meeting
The Delhi Association of Realtors held its monthly meeting on Tuesday, January 18, 19--, at The Heritage Restaurant. The social hour began at 6:00 o'clock, and dinner was served at 7. Seventy-eight of the 85 members were present in addition to four guests.

Call to Order
Immediately following dinner, J. R. Hawkins, president, called the meeting to order and welcomed the members and guests. She noted that the January attendance was 10% above the December attendance.

Approval of Minutes
The minutes were presented by Secretary Tom Phelps. Jim Miller noted that the state convention would be held on the ninth of March instead of on April 10 as stated in the minutes. The correction was made, and the minutes were approved.

Treasurer's Report
In the absence of Susan Peoples, Tom Phelps gave the treasurer's report. The Association has a balance of $1,210 in the treasury, and bills amounting to $75.10 ($35.10 to Rouse Printing Company and $41 to The Heritage Restaurant) are outstanding. An extention of 10 days has been granted to members who haven't paid their dues.

Market Review
Robert Blakenship was called upon to give a summary of the developments that have taken place in the local real estate market. Phelps Real Estate Company has been selected as exclusive marketing agent for Breckenridge subdivision on Leesville Rd. The 79-lot single-family subdivision is a Drexter development. Northwoods Village, a 228-unit luxury apartment community developed by Dallas C. Pickford & Associates, will open on the 1st of August. The community is located at Ten Northwood Village Drive, one-half mile south of Interstate 40.

Speaker
Following the business session, the president introduced Mrs. Sarah Dunbarton, president of Dunbarton Associates, as speaker for the meeting. Mrs. Dunbarton discussed the potential effects of recent tax legislation on the real estate market. She predicted that the prime rate will drop another half point before it hits bottom. In the local area, there will probably be an increase of 12-15 apartment buildings on the market within the next 6 months.

2

Adjournment
Following the presentation, the treasurer drew the lucky number to determine who would win the centerpiece. The lucky number was 320, and winner was Joann Durham.

The meeting was adjourned at 9:15 p.m. Members were reminded that the next meeting would be on the third Tuesday of February.

Respectfully submitted,

Tom Phelps, Secretary

Phelps Real Estate Agency
1125 Umstead Drive Indianapolis, IN 46204-6154 (317) 555-3222

August 19, 19--

Ms. Patricia Strum
One T Kildaire Farm Road
Indianapolis, IN 46205-9241

Dear Ms. Strum

I have some good news for you! The house you are interested in on
thirty-third Street has been reduced $5,000. The price is now within
the range you mentioned to me on the forth. May I urge you to act
quickly.

Because of the favorable mortgage interest rates that are now a
vailable, you can own this 2,200-square-foot house and still have
mortgage payments of less than $900 per month. For a limited time,
the Indianapolis Federal Savings and Loan Association will approve
your application for an adjustable rate loan within 30 days. If
it is not approved, you will not be charged the 1% discount rate.

Please call me at 555-3222 to set up an appointment. My office
hours are from 9:00 to 5 p.m. during the week.

Sincerely

Terry B. Andrus
Agent

df

WALSH PAPERS
2250 Harris Road
Huntsville, AL 35810-2250
(509) 555-5892

June 16, 19--

Ms. Jennifer Elaine Carson
Route 2, Box 507B
Huntsville, AL 35807-8615

PURCHASE ORDER 471
My Dear Ms. Carson

Thank you for your order for six boxes of stationery,
Stock No. 331. The quality of the stationery you have
selected will let your customers know that they are
important to you.

Because of the recent shipping strike, there has been a
delay in our receiving the merchandise from the factory.
We have been informed that the shipment has been sent,
however, and we should receive it within a week. Your
order will be on its way to you as soon as we receive the
shipment. We hope this delay will not inconvenience you
too much.

We appreciate the business you have given us in the past,
and we look forward to serving you in the future.

Sincerely,

Audrey D. Leapley, Manager
Shipping Department

DS   ec
     pc R. P. Michaels

Did the typist make all the necessary changes? **Yes**

a. Ms. Katrina Ann Dewar
    8577 Estate Drive South
    West Palm Beach, FL 33411-9753

    tr Sales Promotion
        Ms Dewar
        Dear Madam

b. Please let me know when we can get together to discuss the
    property.

    Very Sincerely Yours,

    Ms. Donna Raynor

    Enclosure
    ah

c. Carson Real Estate Enterprises
    1860 Memorial Drive
    Greenville, SC 29605-8642

    Ladies and Gentlemen
    Dear Mr. Carson

d. Mr. M. C. Alexander
    1620 Quantico Court
    San Jose, CA 95230-1009

    Dear Mr. M. C. Alexander

e. Ms. Ilo Carlson
    8090 Pinetree Street
    Little Rock, AR 72201-0057

    My Dear Mrs. Carlson

f. Sincerely,

    ds Brian Davis, Manager
    ds dt
        cc Carolyn Walston

The correct placement is shown in Letter **A**.

Internal Memorandum

TO   Associate Editors

FROM Danny Bright, Executive Editor DB

DATE Production Meetings

SUBJECT April 10, 19--

On Monday, April 25, all associate editors should plan to meet in Conference Room C, third floor, at 10 a.m. The purpose of this meeting is to identify topics which are of concern to you as a supervisor.

You are a vital member of our editorial team, and your input is essential to keeping production running smoothly during this very heavy copyright year. Based on your input, we will establish an agenda for future meetings.

re

PERIN OFFICE SYSTEMS
3903 Spaulding Drive
Atlanta, GA 30338-3903
(404) 555-1719

March 17, 19--

Mr. Lloyd Gardner
Vocational Education Director
Tallahassee City Schools
Tallahassee, FL 32308-5489

Dear Mr. Gardner

Thank you for the opportunity to demonstrate our equipment to the office education teachers again this year at the Tallahassee Vocational Drive-In Conference on May 16. Yes, we would be delighted to exhibit.

We think teachers should be particularly interested in the Perin electronic typewriters and our new high-speed desktop copier. We also plan to exhibit the Perin II Personal Computer and a variety of peripherals.

Your description of the exhibit area and available space indicates to me that we would be exhibiting in a prime location, and your charges for this location are equitable. Because we are interested in getting maximum exposure, we are willing to pay the top price. We appreciate your opening the exhibits one hour preceding the first session.

Sincerely yours

Ms. Emily E. Simpson
Regional Manager

mr

PERIN OFFICE SYSTEMS
3903 Spaulding Drive
Atlanta, GA 30338-3903
(404) 555-1719

March 17, 19--

Mr. Roger Moe
Eastman Brothers, Inc.
7861 Monroe Street
Tallahassee, FL 32301-7654

Dear Mr. Moe
Ladies and Gentlemen

Enclosed is a short report reviewing the preliminary design factors that your project committee must consider when planning the 15,000-square-foot addition to your existing facilities.

We will provide complete documentation for these recommendations at our initial planning session on April 7. In the mean time, good luck with your planning.

Sincerely yours

Ms. Emily E. Simpson
Regional Manager

jp

Enclosure

OFFICE DESIGN FACTORS
Eastman Brothers, Inc.

Because office design does affect job performance and job satis faction, several factors should be considered in the preliminary stages of planning the construction or renovation of any facility. This report discusses these factors and gives recommendations which may increase employees' productivity by as much as 30% and decrease absenteeism.

Work Space

The area where workers spend most of their time is their work space. The factors to be considered when work space is designed are discussed below.

Enclosures. The open-office plan with enclosures gives workers the privacy they need, supports communication, and improves productivity more than either the fully open or fully closed office plans. To be effective, the partitions surrounding each work area should be higher than standing height on 3 sides.

Floor area. The amount of usable floor space a worker can call his or her own is based on job need and status. According to recent research (Brill 1985), the minimum requirements for various workers are as follows:

align numerals at right

Managers	115 square feet
Professional/technical workers	82 square feet
Clerical workers	43 square feet

Layout. The physical arrangement (layout) of furniture and walls greatly affects job performance, comfort, status, and ease of communication. Workers should have two good work surfaces and a single front entrance. The layout should be designed so that others are not seated directly in front of the employee.

Lighting

Proper lighting is determined by the quality and quantity of light. The quantity and quality of light affects proper lighting. Approximately 150 fc (footcandles) are recommended for computer usage. Most lighting problems are caused by too much light resulting in glare on documents or reflections on monitors. Although most workers prefer to be near a window, windows do cause glare.

Ambient light fixtures (which illuminate the entire office area) combined with task lighting (which lights specific work surfaces) create the most effective lighting system.

Noise

Office conversations, ringing telephones, and outside noise account for most office noise. Sound-absorbent materials used throughout the building, acoustical enclosures on printers, and layout are effective means of reducing office noise. Office noise should be less than 65 decibels (Casady 1984).

Energy

Energy needs include lines for power, phones, and data. Questions to be answered in determining energy needs are (1) Do you expect high growth in computer usage? and (2) Do you expect to rearrange workstations frequently? how often?

3

Access floors raised of the structural slab provide an excellent solution for distributing heat, air conditioning, and wiring for data and telephone services. These floors have unlimited capacity and may be accessed at any point by service units without calling an electrician. Additionally, quality and speed of transmission will not be affected as your transmission needs grow.

PERIN OFFICE SYSTEMS
3903 Spaulding Drive
Atlanta, GA 30338-3903
(404) 555-1719

From the desk of TERRY ROBERTS

Please check to be sure that I haven't missed any errors. Mr. Holms prefers the modified block letter style with mixed punctuation. Thanks tr

March 17, 19--

Ms Jessica Shimer
2905 Sandcastle Dr.
Tallahassee, FL 32308-9625

Dear Ms. Shimer:

Thank you for your interest in the Perin Laser Copier, Model 212. Enclosed is a brochure detailing its unique features, its specifications, and its cost.

Perin's Laser Copier is the most technologically sophisticated copier on the marked today. This laser-driven copier uses a scanner to digitize originals. Text (including columns) can be manipulated before printing them. Because it is digital, the laser copier can transmit images to other printers and produce high-resolution copiers in seconds.

After you have had a chance to review this brochure, I will give you a call to provide you with additional product or price information or to set up a demonstration. In the meantime, please call me at the number listed above if you have any questions.

Sincerely yours,

Robert C. Holms
Sales Representative

tr

Enclosure

Chapter 6 (continued)   Chapter 7

PERIN OFFICE SYSTEMS   Internal Memorandum

TO: All Product Managers

FROM: Larry Bryant, Systems Manager

DATE: March 17, 19--

SUBJECT: Computer Maintenence

TS

As more and more managers are accessing computer terminals or are acquiring their own, it becomes increasingly important that everyone practice good procedures for operating and maintaining computer terminals and peripherals. Please review these procedures to keep your equipment in good working order.

1. Keep your equipment away from direct sunlight, heat vents, and open windows. Extreme temperatures can damage chips and other components.

2. Keep food and beverages away from equipment and diskettes.

3. Eliminate smoking near equipment. Tobacco smoke contains dust and tars that can damage or clog equipment.

4. Keep paper clips that have been stored in a magnetic container away from diskettes. Keep diskettes away from magnets or any electronic equipment. These items contain magnetic fields that can cause portions of text to be erased.

5. Use anti static mats under your computer. Static electricity can cause memory loss.

6. Never oil your printer or any part of your system. Oil will clog the machine.

7. Check power requirements to be sure your power is sufficent.

8. Do not take anything apart, even if in your judgment you can fix it. Call Helen Mathys (Ext. 278), and she will contact our service representative.

tr

The members of the Lawrence Chamber of Commerce invite you to attend their open house in the new building at 1054 Greene Street on Wednesday, October 23, between the hours of 2 p.m. and 5 p.m.

> The members of the
> Lawrence Chamber of Commerce
> invite you
> to attend their open house
> in the new building at
> 1045 Green Street
> Wednesday, October 23
> between 2 and 5 p.m.

LCC
Lawrence Chamber of Commerce
1054 Greene Street
Lawrence, KS 66044-1000
(316) 555-2361

October 18, 19--

Mr. Charles D. Christian
3162 North Tenth Street
Wichita, KS 67203-9149

Dear Mr. Christian:

We are delighted to send you the information you requested about Queen's Park.

From the map on the enclosed brochure, you can see that the park is divided into 5 areas. The areas includes games and rides, exhibits, live entertainment, concession stands, and a zoo. There is Something for every member of the family to enjoy.

On the enclosed list of rates, you will note that persons under 6 and those over 70 is admitted free. Note, too, that group rates are available.

The park operates on a daily schedule in the summer but is open only on weekends during the spring and fall. Announcements about any special event is placed on the bulletin board at the entrance to the park.

The enclosed pamplet contains a coupon good for $3 off one adult admission ticket. Have fun at Queen's Park!

Yours very truly,

Alex F. Stevens, Director

tr

Enclosures

LCC
Lawrence Chamber of Commerce
1054 Greene Street
Lawrence, KS 66044-1000
(316) 555-2361

February 10, 19--

Ms. Alita Guitterez, President
National Sales Company, Inc.
3910 Trade Street
Lawrence, KN 66044-5133

Dear Ms. Guitterez:

Welcome to Lawrence! We are delighted that your company chose to locate in our city.

As a member of the business community, you are eligible for membership is the Lawrence Chamber of Commerce. On the first Tuesday of each month, we have a breakfast meeting to which each new businessman and businesswoman are invited. This meeting provides an opportunity for us to get to know each other. Each third Tuesday, we have have a dinner and a business meeting at the Arbor Inn.

We hope your schedule will permit you to attend the next meeting, which will be at Tom's Restaurant on the 6th at 7:30 a.m. The Hospitality Committee are in charge of this function. If you can attend, please call 555-2361.

To welcome you as a new member of the business community, Lawrence Chamber of Commerce's newsletter plans to feature a story about your company in our next issue. Will you submit an article of about 500 words about your company? To meet our deadline, we will need the material by the 25th.

Again, welcome to our city!

Very truly yours,

Ms. Cynthia Shepherd, Director
Public Relations

tr

Solutions   221

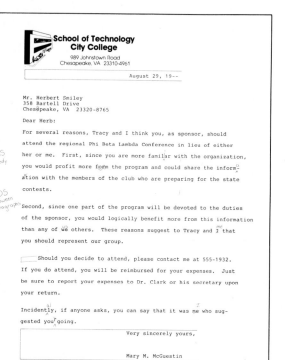

**School of Technology
City College**
989 Johnstown Road
Chesapeake, VA 23310-4961

August 29, 19--

Mr. Herbert Smiley
358 Bartell Drive
Chesapeake, VA 23320-8765

Dear Herb:

For several reasons, Tracy and I think you, as sponsor, should attend the regional Phi Beta Lambda Conference in lieu of either her or me. First, since you are more familar with the organization, you would profit more form the program and could share the information with the members of the club who are preparing for the state contests.

Second, since one part of the program will be devoted to the duties of the sponsor, you would logically benefit more from this information than any of we others. These reasons suggest to Tracy and I that you should represent our group.

Should you decide to attend, please contact me at 555-1932. If you do attend, you will be reimbursed for your expenses. Just be sure to report your expenses to Dr. Clark or his secretary upon your return.

Incidently, if anyone asks, you can say that it was me who suggested you going.

Very sincerely yours,

Mary M. McGuestin

RV

**School of Technology
City College**

Internal Memorandum

TO: All Staff
FROM: Brian Layman, Dean
DATE: August 29, 19--
SUBJECT: Establishment of Task Force

At the suggestion of numerous staff members, the university is pursuing the idea of purchasing a computer system for general use. Members of the staff with who I have talked have shown many applications for computer useage in your daily work.

A task force of interested staff members are being formed to conduct a more through study of the needs of the staff. Based on its findings, the task force will then make recommendations for the purchase of a computer system and software. I need to know who among the staff are interested in serving on the task force.

Responsibilities of the task force includes the following: (1) assessing the staff's needs, (2) gathering information about computer systems, (3) evaluating the software available, and (4) to make recommendations to the purchasing agent and I.

If your interested in actively researching this topic and meeting this challenge, please send me a memo indicating your interest.

rv

**School of Technology
City College**

Internal Memorandum

TO: Department Chairpersons
FROM: Brian Layman, Dean
DATE: August 29, 19--
SUBJECT: Parking Regulations

In an effort to improve staff parking conditions, the Campus Traffic Committee have developed the following parking regulations. Will you please see that all members of your department receives this information regarding the new regulations.

1. All current campus parking permits expire on September 14. Beginning September 15, new permits are required for we staff members.

2. Parking is prohibited in areas other then those designated for staff members.

3. Parking is prohibited in metered areas.

4. Parking regulations must be observed in locations where specific hours are listed.

5. Permanent premits must be displayed in the rear window of all vechicles.

6. Campus security officers will issue tickets to those who violate the parking regulations.

Because Chief Security Officer Calder has been aware of the miscellaneous problems in parking, he was very receptive to the recommendations made by the staff members who comprised the committee. In fact, it was him who suggested a number of the new regulations.

Department Chairpersons
Page 2
August 29, 19--

Officer Calder and the members of the Traffic Committee is sure that the members of your department, as responsable college employees, will cooperate by adhering to these regulations. If you become aware of any criticism of the new regulations, please let me know--the college administration welcomes and recognizes employee comments and suggestions.

rv

Chapter 9

Hartsell Real Estate   Internal Memorandum

TO: Hannah Silverthorne

FROM: Walter T. Hartsell

DATE: July 14, 19--

SUBJECT: Sales Quota Exceeded

Congratulations on your success not only in reaching but also (past) in exceeding your sales quota for the passed six months. In view of the sluggish market during this period, I realize it's taken alot of personal effort to reach this goal.

Your performance demonstrates that you believe in the principle that what is good for business is good for you. Cold canvassing is never easy, but your attitude shows that your objective is to sell property, not to avoid failure--to gain valuable experience, not to maintain the status quo. The net affect of your efforts are that we will not loose our No. 1 ranking in the city.

Thank you, Hannah, for your contributions; your enthusasm is contagious. I'm proud to have you on our sales force.

yri

Hartsell Real Estate
1760 Asbury Street
Indianapolis, IN 46203-3952

July 19, 19--

Mr. Bryant Whitehurst
Plant Manager
Toggs Manufacturing Co.
P. O. Box 7022
Indianapolis, IN 46208-9865

Dear Mr. Whitehurst:

The one hundred-acre sight on Five-Mile Rd. you wanted for your new plant is available. Even though the owners have all ready had a lot of inquiries about the property, I believe they're prepared to accept your proposed offer.

If you are serious about obtaining this property, I suggest that you submit an offer immediately. Real estate prices are not likely to decrease further this year. In fact, it is likely to increase.

Because the owners insist on a cash transaction, you may want to get your counsel's advise about the best way to finance the principal loan. Please call me to discuss your plans about this matter.

Sincerely yours,

Walter T. Hartsell
General Manager

yri

Hartsell Real Estate
1760 Asbury Street
Indianapolis, IN 46203-3952

July 14, 19--

Miss Kimary Etheridge
Personnel Director
Merritt Electronic Co.
7643 Evans Avenue
Gainesville, Florida 32612-9876

Dear Ms. Kimary:

I was surprised to learn that Ms. Melanie Cooke has used my name as a referance on her application for a job with your company.

Ms. Cooke worked with me for about 3 months. During that time her work was never up to the standards demanded by business. My major criticasm of her as an employee centered on her carelessness and inefficiency in her work.

Ms. Cooke frequently arrived late or left early. She was careless in her personel appearance, and her overall attitude was not good. After speaking to her on several occassions about her lack of efficiency and then noting no improvement, I was forced to dismiss her.

Had Ms. Cooke requested permission to use my name as a referance, I would have declined; but since she did not, I have no alternative but to give her an unsatisfactory recommendation.

Sincerely yours,

Walter T. Hartsell
General Manager

yri

Chapter 10

McDowell Travel Agency

4500 West Kennedy Boulevard • Tampa, FL 33609-3421 • (800) 555-2435

October 25, 19--

Col. Edward C. Barrett
1100 Madison (Ave.) sp
Goldsboro, NC 27530-8959

Dear (Col.) Barrett

Thank you for your letter of October 15 requesting brochures,
price lists, and information sheets about cruises leaving from
Miami, (FL) sp Your inquiry comes at a time when there are a
number of interesting, exotic cruises at fabulously low
prices.

I have requested that three cruise lines send you up-to-date
information about their winter cruises, and I am sure you
will hear from them soon. Consider each line's total cost
the cost of air travel to the point of departure, and the
itinerary when you are making a choice. You will note that
prices for a seven-day cruise range from $625 to $1800 per
person.

I have enclosed information about choosing a cruise that I
hope will be helpful. After you make your desicion about
the cruise, fill out and return the data sheet. You can
then leave everything in our hands and rest assured that
satisfactory arrangements will be made.

We look forward to serving as your liaison with the cruise
line of your choice and to assist you in any way possible.

Sincerely

Mrs. Laura E. Spellman
Marketing Manager

os

Enclosures

PERSONAL DATA SHEET

Name_____

Address_____

Spouse (if any)_____

Cruise No._____
Destination_____

Departure Date_____

Return Date_____

Insurance Desired   Yes_____
                    No_____

Name of Person to Call in Case of Emergency_____
                    Telephone Number_____

FOR OFFICE USE ONLY: LAST NAME:_____
                      SHIP NO._____ RECEIPT NO._____

CHOOSING THE RIGHT CRUISE FOR YOU

As the winter cruise season approaches, discounts on ship fares are plentiful in the travel industry, and smart consumers are taking advantage of the special bargains. Now is the time to consider taking a leisurely cruise if it is one of those things that will fulfill a lifetime dream for you. If you have never pictured yourself as a passenger on a cruise ship, consider the facts given below.

Passenger Profile

Once cruises were a pastime for the rich and the retired. Today cruises are taken by individuals from all walks of life and all income levels. Forty-eight percent of cruise passengers now earn less than $25,000 a year. Nearly half are under forty-five years of age, and ten percent are under twenty-five.

It is estimated that more than a million and a half people will take cruises on about one hundred cruise ships this year, and cruise lines are competitively vying for this business. Two qualities of the cruise experience are being stressed: value and convenience. Now is a great time to participate in what some refer to as the "cruise revolution."

Cost and Convenience

Consider the price of the average cruise. The price that you pay includes accommodations, baggage handling, meals, entertainment (including first-run movies and live performances), room service, daily activities ranging from computer lessons to disco dancing, travel to any number of ports, and reduced air fare from home.

2

Convenience is another factor that you must consider as you contemplate taking a cruise. In what other way can you travel from one country to another without having to unpack and repack your bags? Where else can you spend days or weeks without having to open your wallet or purse constantly? You don't even have to worry about arranging travel schedules, making plane reservations, or waiting long hours in airports.

Activities on Board

To be sure that your cruise proves to be all that you expect it to be, you should take the time to find out what the various cruise lines offer and to whom they cater. For example, some cruise lines cater to children and make special provisions for them. Other lines cater only to adults. Some provide for academic pursuits while others primarily provide entertainment and recreation.

You should give some thought to the types of activities that you might enjoy. Do you want entertainment? Do you want some physical fitness programs? Do you want to learn something? There is at least one cruise ship that doubles on a regular basis as a floating university. There is no pressure to participate in any of the activities provided by the cruise line. If you wish, you can relax on the deck with a book or watch television in your own cabin. You can choose your own recreation.

Cruise Itinerary

Another important criteria that will affect your selection of a cruise is the planned itinerary of the ship. Consider the number of stops you would be making and the ports you would be visiting. Are there particular cities you have always wanted to tour?

3

Your travel agent can provide you with a detailed list of port choices and itinerary options to help you decide on the best cruise.

How to Get Started

After you have made some of the major decisions regarding your preferences in a cruise, see your travel agent. The agent can help determine which cruise suits your needs and provide answers to any other questions that you might have. In other words, your travel agent is the liaison between you and the cruise line. Using a travel agent is the best way to take the worry out of traveling. Contact your travel agent today.

Chapter 11

The Jackson Herald

DESKTOP PUBLISHING

A New Concept in Document Production

What is desktop publishing? Why is it capturing the attention of so many people? Will it revolutionize the appearance of documents? Will it become the standard way to produce ads and brochures? to produce all corporate communications?

Although some of these questions may remain unanswered for some time one thing is sure: Desktop publishing is definitely changing the communication process for a number of organizations.

What Is Desktop Publishing?

Desktop publishing describes the process by which a professional quality document is produced using a microcomputer system and a special software. It thus enables the production of typeset-quality pages in-house.

IS WYSIWYG FOR YOU?

Software

WYSIWIG, which stands for "What you see is what you get," characterizes much of the composition software. WYSIWYG (pronounced "wissy wig") means that what you see on the screen is exactly what you'll get when the copy is printed. Headlines appear in large and bold type, italics appear slanted, and vertical spacing appears as it will when printed.

Copy can be spread between columns on a page and multiple headings being used on a page.

Printer

Although a dot matrix printer can be utilized, laser printers facilitate the use of multiple type sizes and styles on the same page. Graphics such as letterheads and logos, free-hand drawings (done with a mouse), and scanned images such as photographs or drawings may be integrated with copy.

"Desktop publishing may replace word processing software for final output."

Is There a Market?

Yesterday's "paperless" office is becoming today's "paperful" office. Experts tell us that the average office worker had to read 900 pages of hard copy per month last year, and this figure is increasing by ten to fifteen percent each year. Utilization of paper as the major means of communicating is likely to be with us for a long time.

Traditionally, offices have depended upon two types of paper communications: (1) typewriter output and (2) typeset output. Until recently, professional-quality printing was limited to the domain of graphic arts professionals: typesetters, pasteup artists, and printers. Desktop publishing enables typeset-quality pages to be produced in-house. With a little practice, and some good design ideas, managers, office workers, or students can create their own layouts complete with borders, rules, columns of type, and other graphic elements.

How Is It Used?

As shown from a questionnaire sent to over ninety users, people are using desktop systems for an array of different purposes: ads, brochures, business forms, manuals, proposals, newsletters, resumes, and transparency masters.

Ms. Julie Newton, vice president of a publishing consulting firm, predicts that desktop publishing will even replace word processing software for final output. One consultant commented, "Once you start producing professional looking pages, your audience will get used to it."

The potential of desktop publishing remains to be seen. Certainly it is providing a likable alternative to using outside typesetters for business publications.

"Once you start producing professional looking pages, your audience will get used to it."

This handout on desktop publishing was prepared by Kim Stephens. For more information on desktop publishing systems call her at Extension 212.

DOES DESKTOP PUBLISHING PAY?
HERE'S WHAT THEY SAY

The expansion of desktop publishing is now a certainty. Today's decision makers would do well to stop, look, and listen to what users of desktop publishing systems are saying.

If "time is money," consider the money that can be saved by eliminating the turnaround time involved in producing documents through outside suppliers. A national car rental agency enjoyed increased revenues of 10% to 12% because it was able to produce price lists weekly in-house as compared to every three weeks using an outside source. Time was saved, and price lists were current.

A San Francisco photographer who was relocating to New York designed and produced personal letterhead stationary and appropriate business cards in three hours using his computer.

Ambitious students are using these desktop systems to produce term papers. Consequently, students who do not have access to composition software are complaining that they are at a disadvantage. Some professors have ruled that, while neatness counts, typeset term papers are just a little too neat.

An editor in charge of creating a 250-page software manual wanted it to appear typeset. The estimates for an outside typesetter and printer were approximately $10,000. She was able to purchase an entire system (computer, software, and printer) for slightly more than the printing costs of this one job.

Paul Brainerd, developer of the Page-Maker program, stated that publishing has come full circle. After Gutenberg, the publisher was also the printer--right in his own shop. Now the publisher can once again do the printing on his desktop.

MARY, WE'VE FOUND THE ANSWER TO REDUCING PUBLISHING COSTS. IT'S IN-HOUSE PUBLISHING... ON A PC.

THAT LOOKS GREAT, JIM. BUT WHAT KIND OF SOFTWARE ARE YOU USING?

WYSIWYG

HERE'S THE ANSWER, MARY! TOTAL-PAGE SOFTWARE!

For more information, fill in the coupon below. Upon receipt of your inquiry, we will send you information about the newest thing in desktop publishing software, the TOTAL-PAGE.

Name _____ Title _____

Company _____

Address _____

(city) (state) (zip)

Mail to: The Upjohn Software Company
1010 Rives Street
Baltimore, MA 21226-2318

Chapter 12

Maryland Farm Association

1920 Sherwood Road   Baltimore, MD 21227-5057

TO: Farm Association Members

FROM: Tim Jenkins, President

DATE: April 10, 19--

SUBJECT: Membership Renewal

No one knows the needs of the farmer better than the farmer. Through the years, the Farm Association has been the voice of farmers from coast to coast.

The Farm Association continues to be an influential voice for agriculture. The Associations passed record in legislatures nationwide is evidence of this influence: Thirty farm bills were introduced in state legislatures within the last year.

The achievments of the Association are due to policy developments at the local, state, and national level. The most noticable strength of the organization is at the local level, because thats where policies originate and action begins.

With the number of farmers decreasing each year, we must exert extra effort to retain existing members by strengthening involvement, particularly at the local level. Paralleling this effort, we must strive to enroll new members.

Show your commitment to the success of agriculture by following these steps--1) fill in the membership renewal form, 2) attach your check for $25, and 3) dropping your letter in the mailbox. It could be--and probably will be--the best investment you will ever make.

sf

Maryland Farm Association

1920 Sherwood Road   Baltimore, MD 21227-5057

Date Missing

Mr. Clifton Everett, President
Iowa Farm Association
689 Hazel Street
Boise, IO 83702-3782

Dear Mr. Everett

When the Planning Committee for the Maryland Farm Association, (MFA) State Convention met to plan next years convention, you were unamously chosen to be the keynote speaker. We hope you will be able to accept our invitation--and this is your invitation--to be with us.

The MFA Convention is scheduled for November 17-19 at the Radisson Hotel in Baltimore, your presentation would be at 10 a.m. on November 18.

Our members are extremely concerned about the increasing number of bankruptcies, 72 in our state this year. We would like you to share your analsis of the recent legislation that is having a crucial affect upon farmers, and outline a plan for financial farm management. Please mention strategies for handling debtor obligations prudently. You could, for example, outline the financial assistants available to farmers, however, you may choose your own topic. Members who have heard you speak report that your explanations are extremely clear, and your delivery is superb.

If you agree to be our keynote speaker on November 18, we will pay you an honorarium of $200.00, and we will pay travel, meal, and lodging expenses. Please let us know within 2 weeks whether you can be our speaker.

Sincerely

Corey B. Dupree
State Convention Committee

sf

WHAT IS HAPPENING TO RURAL AMERICA?

To city dwellers, the word rural brings certain things to mind, rolling hills and picturesque barns, pickup trucks and loaded hay wagons, limited employment opportunities, and a population on the decline. On the contrary, rural America is changing. The population involved in agriculture-related businesses are growing.

A report prepared by the Dept. of Ag. analyzed 2,443 nonmetropolitan counties--those that make up rural America--and found that the population has increased over a 10-year period by 16 percent--nearly twice the rate of metroplitan countries.

Out of a total of 2,442,702 (less than 29 percent) of the nonmetropolitan counties are dominated by farming. Consider the fact that only one out of every forty people today actually lives on the farm. 55 years ago one fourth of Americans lived on farms.

One might naturally ask, "Why then is the population of rural America growing?" Today there are many more individuals engaged in getting farm products to the consumer. They include farm suppliers, transportation workers, wholesalers and retailers; chefs, waiters, and waitresses; and cashiers and office workers engaged in these businesses.

Including those individuals engaged in providing products and services that are farm-related, U. S. agriculture employs about 23 million people. These individuals supply the 714 meals (and snacks) that are consumed in the U. S. each day--a gastronomical figure!

Although the number of Americans living on farms today has decreased, more Americans than ever before are closely associated with rural America. Rural America is still making an impact that is felt across the nation.

 NEWS RELEASE

AMERICAN BUSINESS EDUCATION ASSOCIATION
1111 South Wabash Street
Chicago, Il. 60605-2912

Release Date: February 28, 19--

Over two thousand A.B.E.A. members are expected to converge on Miami, Florida, when the American business education association's thirty-eighth annual convention convenes on March 13. This information comes from Dr. Sue D. Briley, President of the ABEA. Dr. Briley, a business education instructor at Parks College, is serving the first year of a two-year term as President.

Using the theme "Get In Touch With The Future," Dr. Briley and her convention committee have planned a program featuring numerous leaders in the business education areas of Accounting, Computer Science, Keyboarding, and Economics.

Approximately 125 textbook publishers and equipment salespeople are expected to exhibit their products.

The entertainment committee has succeeded in getting well-known Motivational Speaker Zig Ziglar for the luncheon presentation. Internationally famous entertainer Danny Kaye will provide entertainment at the closing banquet. The committee has also planned a jamboree for the 15th of March at the Orange Bowl.

The convention will end with a business session on the 17th of March.

Dr. M. Ellen Schwartz

WHERE TO GO AND WHAT TO SEE IN MIAMI IN MARCH

Miami has some especially fascinating activities scheduled for Mid-March, when ABEA members will be in town. Selected events listed in this week in Miami, a weekly magazine published by the Miami chamber of commerce are as follows.

1. The Annual Shakespeare festival (March 5-23). Three of the great bard's plays are being presented: Two gentlemen of Verona, Romeo and Juliet, and the Tempest.
2. The Dade County Counsel of arts folk festival (March 15-16). Featured will be local artists and craftspeople. Admission is free.
4. Violinist Itzhak Perlman Concert (March 17). To reserve tickets, call (305) 555-3491.

In addition to these special attractions, the following year-round activities are available:

Vizcaya. It was a great Italian villa located on Biscayne bay. Built by James Deering in 1916. Admission is $5 for adults and $3.50 for children under 12.

Shoping centers. Two fine ones are mayfair mall, a high-fashion boutique center, and miracle mile, a four-block shopping extravaganza in Coral Gables.

Bus tours and harbor cruises. Check at your hotel desk for details.

To travel outside the city, you might consider renting a Century or Thrifty car and traveling North to fort Lauderdale or South to Key West. You can take highway 1 to each of these cities.

 abea

AMERICAN BUSINESS EDUCATION ASSOCIATION
1111 South Wabash Street
Chicago, Il. 60605-2912

January 13, 19--

Dr. Peggy Martin, professor
School of Business Education
Eastern University
1072 East 5th Street
Charleston, IL

Dear Dr. Martin:

Make your plans now to head South in late Winter to attend the American Business Education assoc iation's annual convention. The Palms hotel in Miami, FL will be the site for this 38th meeting, which begins on March 13 and ends on March 17.

"Get In Touch With The Future" is the theme of this year's convention. Several new, pertinent topics have been added, one of which is "Experimental Learning--The Educational Tool for the Future."

Send your hotel registration directly to the Palms Hotel, 2500 Third Avenue, S.W., Miami, FL 33129-0615, no later than February 28 to ensure a room at the convention hotel. You may guarantee your reservation by including your Am. express card number.

To register for the convention, complete the registration form that is in the December issue of the ABEA journal. Mail it along with your check to this office by Feb. 15.

Plan to attend the opening session followed by the Orange Bowl Jamboree; a watch containing a miniature TV will be given away as a door prize.

Please extend an invitation to students, and emphasize the value of participating in a conference designed for professional growth.

Very Truly Yours,

M. Ellen Schwartz

AA

Chapter 14

TOPS
(Temporary Office Personnel Services)
909 Linden Avenue
New Orleans LA 70128-9400

August 15, 19--

Ms. Mary Dunstan
2001 King Alfred Drive
Baton Rogue, LO 71304-6421

Dear Ms. Dunstan

Since you asked me to make suggestions for improving the efficiency
of TOPS, I am writing to share with you an idea that I believe
will have a very positive effect on the productivity of this office.
I am eager to hear your reaction.

Recently I had the opportunity to examine a new publication from
South-Western Publishing Company entitled Programmed Proofreading.
I believe we should ask each temporary office employee to work
through this publication before beginning an actual assignment with
us. The payoff in productivity and accuracy will, in my opinion,
be well worth the cost of the books.

At the present time, I am spending quite a bit of time proofreading
the documents produced by our employees. Many of the errors that
I rather frequently find are addressed in the book. Working through
exercises that contain those errors will impress upon our employees
the importance of absolute accuracy. While I would continue to
proofread the documents, I believe my proofreading time would
be cut considerably.

There are thirteen chapters in the Programmed Proofreading book.
I found Chapter 12 on content errors to be especially helpful.

Sincerely

Charles Daniels

JP

IS FLEXPLACE IN YOUR VOCABULARY?

Some years ago, many organizations adopted "flextime," making
it possible, beyond a shadow of a doubt, for employees to juggle
work schedules and home responsibilites. At this point in time,
there is flexplace (sometimes referred to as "telecommute").

What Is "Flexplace"?

The flexplace arrangement enables employees to do all or part
of their work away from the corporate office. Various forms of
decentralized workplaces are possible, satellite offices, or
branch offices that are linked electronically to main offices,
neighborhood offices that are shared by employees of different
companies, and employees' homes.

For Whom is It Designed?

Flexplace is best implemented in information-intensive firms
that have computers, networks, and data bases installed: banks,
insurance companies, and financial institutions. Managers and
professionals who work independently, as well as computer specialists,
and women who are secretaries, and data entry specialists are best
suited for flexplace. Consider these cases:

Disabled from a severe accident, Leslie Longhill works at
home as a program analyst; her computer is linked by phone lines
to clients' computers and to her companies computer. Allan and
Lorraine Templeton operate a consulting business for a large cor-
poration. Loraine also works part-time as a programmer for a
large corporation. A typesetting firm employs Janet Gabor to

2

meet its fluctuating needs. Jane, mother of three young children,
burns the candle at both ends because she is also fulfilling
family responsibilities.
Advantages of Flexplace

Some employers consider flexplace as a way to reduce costs,
to attract personal whom would not otherwise be available for
employment, and increasing productivity. A large insurance company estimated that 16 home-based persons produced 50 percent more
than persons working at the office. Another computer company reported a 35 percent increase in productivity.

In this day and age when people are seeking an alternative
to the high costs and frustrations of commuting to work, many
persons consider that the freedom of workplace may be an important
benefit. Flextime enables persons who are self-motivated, on the
ball, and who manage their time well to work independantly. However, caution must be exercised that working at home doesn't
become all work and no play. Working at home can create additional
stress by making it impossible to escape the demands of the office.

Conclusion

Is flexplace for you? Despite the fact that it may not be
feasible or possible for all workers, it may be appropriate for
others. Research and experimentation by organizations that are
willing to establish "telework" arrangements will reveal whether
or not flexible working arrangements are viable.

STRETCH YOUR TRAVEL DOLLAR

The cost of obtaining money to travel abroad is often over-
looked in travel budgets. Here are some important essential
tips for those planning to travel abroad soon:

☞ Plan your needs carefully to avoid making unnecessary
exchanges. Estimate how much you want to put on credit
cards. Then buy traveler's checks for the balance. There
is usually a one percent fee to buy traveler's checks and
another 1 to 4 percent fee to convert them into foreign
currency. The service charge for credit card transactions
can cause you to spend an additional 1 to 7 percent on
money exchange.

☞ Look for the best deal on traveler's checks. You usually
pay twice when you use traveler's checks--when you buy
them and when you convert them. Try to find an outlet
that does not impose a sales charge.

☞ Consider the value of the dollar. In the event that the
dollar declines, it will buy less. If you think the value
of the dollar will decrease before you take your trip,
consider prepaid tour packages so that costs will remain
stable. Traveler's checks issued in foreign currency
provide another safeguard against a weakening dollar.

☞ Consider using European Currency Units. ECUs consit of
10 common market currencies and are accepted in countries
where traveler's checks are accepted. They are sold at
some european banks and at european offices of Am. Express.

☞ Choose credit cards wisely. A travel agent can advice
you, but you must decide whether his advice meets your
needs. Travel and entertainment cards offer the best

2

services for travelers who run short of cach, but the
annual fees are higher. Some Credit Cards offer revolving
credit and have lower service fees, but interest is charged
if cash advances are made. A recent survey of issuing
banks showed a range in interest rates from 12.5% to 21%--
a difference of 7.5 percent. It at all times pays to shop
around.

☞ Compare exchange costs. The best choices for exchange
are large banks; they usually offer better rates than
airports and railroad stations. You will usually find
a good exchange rate from the company that issued your
traveler's checks.

☞ Protect your cash and your credit cards. Exchangeing several
small traveler's checks is expensive and costly, but that
cost must be weighed against the disadvantage of carrying
more cash. You may be interested in investing in a wallet
made especially for traveling. Some hang around the neck;
others go around the waist. Safeguard your credit cards
by making photocopies of it before you leave.

☞ Spend your coins wisely. Although easier said than done,
use your foreign coins before you leave each country, since
they can't be converted. Finally, keep enough American
dollars to get you home safely.

Posttest Solution

Posttest

Proofread each of the following sentences, and use proofreading symbols to indicate changes that should be made. If a sentence is correct, write "C" after it. Solutions to the Posttest begin on page 231.

1. Each report will require six sheets of 8½- by 11-inch paper. C
2. After welcoming faculty and students, the revised schedule was distibuted.
3. As you travel north on interstate 55 to Los Angeks, turn off at the Vine Ave. exit.
4. An embarrasing article about the company in a computre trade publication.
5. Lynn and Dawn was in band practice at South high school for three hours.
6. Keyboardin and listening skills continues to be prerequites for office employees
7. The criteria for entering the contest has been changed.
8. Neither Jerry nor Bob have the diskettes he needs for the FORTRAN class.
9. Here is the insturctions: Every desk and chair has to be removed from the offices.
10. Everybody was pleased that the number of late registrants were smaller than before.
11. If Doctor Chas. Wrenn, an officer in the A. M. A., takes flight 128 at 12 noon, E. S. T., he will arrive in Portland at 1 p.m. PST.
12. Jade objects found in China included pendants bracelets and hairpins.
13. All salespeople on the team did their jobs well. C
14. The team voted to hold their practice session on Friday night.
15. Have you and her decided whether to take Spanish or Accounting next fall?
16. Chris is the one whom will receive the award.
17. Keith had neither completed the payroll nor making a deposit, but the company mailed it's monthly report on Wenesday anyway.
18. Mr. C. R. Lewis, business manager, is working on his m.b.a. at Tulane University.
19. It will take us about twenty-five years to repay the principal on our home mortgage. C
20. The capital of New Mexico, Santa Fe, is located in the north-central part of the state. C
21. The waiter brought French dressing, but I had ordered Italian dressing. C
22. You should notify our Personnel Department prior to a planed absence.
23. Mark won a Zenith color television. C
24. The UPI reported that Ex-President Ford is planning a campaign tour of the Southwest.
25. Information about the winter conference is on page 18 of section 3 of today's paper.
26. The article was sent by federal express on Nov. 10 and it reached the governor on the 11th.
27. The committee sent a terse reminder to the 8 people, who were delinquent.
28. Look! That house is on fire!
29. About 500 more studnets are enrolled in the class—an increase of eight percent.
30. I would prefer someone, who has had experience with an environmental agency.
31. The article "Should I By Gold and Silver Now?" contains some very good references, including the book "Investing in Metals and Coins."
32. Gloria's telephone number appeared as 555-455.
33. All of the subscription money had been turned in, and Chairman Volpe offered congradulations for a job well done.
34. Jane Maier said, " I proofread the letter and did not find an error.
35. On January 10, 1988, Stewart Mays, President of Baldwin College, will present a lecture entitled The Benefits of Desktop Publishing."
36. Your deposit will be refunded by the fifteenth of April, of course; but you must make your request be March 31st.
37. I am sending the material by certified mail, return receipt requested.
38. Announcements of the meeting were sent to the following people: Timothy Cloud, director of production; Annette Pilgreen, director of marketing, and Susan Stansbury, director of sales.
39. The advise "Get hooked on Seafood" seems to be scientifically sound.
40. It was a long, hot, humid summer; therefore, we spent alot of time at the beach.
41. The doors open at 9 o'clock, so I'll meet you for coffee at 10.
42. When you receive the letter, sign your name on the enclosed form, attach your check for $15.50, and send the form and check to me.
43. Dial 555-8111 and give (1) your name, (2) your address, (3) your telephone number, and (4) your date of birth.
44. Begin your exercize plan by swimming a moderate number of laps (15) and then rest.
45. A copy of the original Declaration of Independence—the 22d to be located—was found in North Carolina in 1983 and sold at an auction for $135,000.00.
46. In slow, measured tones, General Harnett read the famous document to a gatherin of 3,250 people.
47. A panda cub, which weighed 3½ ounces at berth, was born to a bear weighing 237 pounds.
48. Will you refer to Chapter 15, Page 13, for the story of the farmer's plight.
49. Did you know that in 1986, 20 of 150 people failed the law examination?
50. If the first line of a letter address is "Ms. Louise Forehand," the salutation should be "Dear Ms. Forhand," not "Dear Madam."

Appendix

FREQUENTLY MISSPELLED WORDS

absence	conscientious	fascinate	miscellaneous	quantity
accommodate	conscious	February	mortgage	questionnaire
accumulate	consensus	fluctuating	necessary	receipt
achievement	convenience	foreign	nickel	receiving
acknowledgment	copyright	fourth	ninety	recognize
amateur	criticism	fulfill	ninth	recommendation
analysis	debtor	grammar	noticeable	reference
analyst	decision	gratitude	occasionally	regard
analyze	definitely	guarantee	occurrence	relevant
announcement	description	height	omitted	repetition
apologize	development	immediately	opportunity	responsible
appropriate	efficiency	implemented	pamphlet	restaurant
approximately	eligible	incidentally	parallel	schedule
bankruptcy	eliminate	independent	particularly	separate
beginning	embarrass	insistent	permanent	similar
believe	emergency	insurance	permissible	strictly
brochure	emphasize	integrate	perseverance	sufficient
bulletin	enthusiasm	itinerary	possession	transferred
calendar	environment	judgment	precede	unanimous
category	equipped	knowledge	prerequisite	undoubtedly
changeable	exaggerate	leisure	privilege	usable
column	experience	liaison	procedure	utilization
commitment	explanation	license	productivity	valuable
committee	extension	maintenance	profited	volume
concession	facilitate	merchandise	programmer	waive
congratulations	familiar	miniature	psychology	writing

COMMONLY MISSPELLED U.S. CITIES

Abilene, TX
Albuquerque, NM
Amarillo, TX
Anaheim, CA
Anchorage, AK
Baltimore, MD
Baton Rouge, LA
Berkeley, CA
Birmingham, AL or MI
Bismarck, ND
Boise, ID
Butte, MT
Charlotte, NC
Chattanooga, TN
Chesapeake, VA
Cheyenne, WY
Chicago, IL
Cincinnati, OH

Des Moines, IA
Detroit, MI
Dubuque, IA
Durham, NC
El Paso, TX
Erie, PA
Fayetteville, NC or AR
Fort Lauderdale, FL
Fresno, CA
Gainesville, FL or GA
Honolulu, HI
Houston, TX
Indianapolis, IN
Kalamazoo, MI
Laramie, WY
Las Vegas, NV
Lincoln, NE
Los Angeles, CA

Louisville, KY
Memphis, TN
Miami, FL
Milwaukee, WI
Minneapolis, MN
Montgomery, AL
Montpelier, VT
Newark, CA, DE, NJ, or OH
New Orleans, LA
Norfolk, VA or NB
Omaha, NE
Pasadena, CA or TX
Philadelphia, PA
Phoenix, AZ
Pittsburgh, PA
Poughkeepsie, NY
Racine, WI
Raleigh, NC

Roanoke, VA
Sacramento, CA
St. Louis, MO
San Antonio, TX
San Bernardino, CA
San Diego, CA
San Francisco, CA
San Jose, CA
Santa Fe, NM
Savannah, GA
Schenectady, NY
Shreveport, LA
Sioux City, IA
Syracuse, NY
Tallahassee, FL
Tucson, AZ
Wichita, KS
Worcester, MA

STATE, DISTRICT, AND TERRITORY ABBREVIATIONS

Alabama, AL
Alaska, AK
Arizona, AZ
Arkansas, AR
American Samoa, AS
California, CA
Colorado, CO
Connecticut, CT
Delaware, DE
District of Columbia, DC
Florida, FL
Georgia, GA
Guam, GU
Hawaii, HI
Idaho, ID
Illinois, IL
Indiana, IN
Iowa, IA
Kansas, KS

Kentucky, KY
Louisiana, LA
Maine, ME
Maryland, MD
Massachusetts, MA
Michigan, MI
Minnesota, MN
Mississippi, MS
Missouri, MO
Montana, MT
Nebraska, NE
Nevada, NV
New Hamsphire, NH
New Jersey, NJ
New Mexico, NM
New York, NY
North Carolina, NC
North Dakota, ND
No. Mariana Islands, CM

Ohio, OH
Oklahoma, OK
Oregon, OR
Pennsylvania, PA
Puerto Rico, PR
Rhode Island, RI
South Carolina, SC
South Dakota, SD
Tennessee, TN
Trust Territories, TT
Texas, TX
Utah, UT
Vermont, VT
Virginia, VA
Virgin Islands, VI
Washington, WA
West Virginia, WV
Wisconsin, WI
Wyoming, WY